Mommy when
I was big

Mommy when I was big

The journey home

Trish Avery

Rev. date: 10/29/2020

To order additional copies of this book, contact:
Xlibris
844-714-8691
www.Xlibris.com
Orders@Xlibris.com
794588

It is in telling the story that we find out who we really are.

CONTENTS

PREFACE

THIS BOOK IS the third book in my Awakening series, taking us full circle in our journey through the circle of life. The circle of life connects the dots in our personal story to our purpose, outlining our journey to the source. I use the words *highly sensitive* and *empath* throughout this book, and for the purposes of this book, they are meant to be the same.

The main questions I get asked all the time are as follows: "What is my purpose?" "Why am I here?" "If everything happens for a reason, what is the reason?" "How do I find these answers?" This book explores these questions, helping you find the purpose and meaning of the journey of life, awakening you to your own personal journey, connecting the dots to your own story coming full circle as you journey home. By hearing the stories of our children, we can start to open our eyes to the possibilities that lie in our own journey.

Our children are our innocence. They have no human agenda, and although they have so much to learn about the earthly plane they have so recently traveled into, they hold so much wisdom from the time before they traveled here, before they chose you as their parents. This is just another grade that they have advanced to in this earth school of so many lessons as they evolve and ascend to where the soul has learned its lessons, has full awareness of its spiritual nature, has no karma (good or bad) to fulfill, and has merged with its higher self. Some call this God or the divine. Here, they can choose to reincarnate (or not) as teachers.

We start in this book with the soul because that is where it all begins. On this journey, I will show you how to recognize the wisdom of your child as he or she tells you about their journey. Some children only remember bits and pieces, and others remember more. Each has validity within this journey and could hold the keys to our own personal journey as well, for it is believed that we travel in our own personal circles of life. I will also take you through the Akashic records, where all our lives are stored, and then to reincarnation and past lives. I will tell true stories of children who remember their previous lives and the signs that they show us early in life as well as how this all links our soul to the circle of life and our journey home. Children remember their past lives without pretense. They see it as if reincarnation is a way wherein the soul moves throughout time from one journey to the next. They know that each past-life memory is a segment in their continuing journey and the evolution of the soul.

I wrote this book because with all that has changed through the generations, I have encountered more and more people who are searching for answers that have not been sought through the mainstream ways of life. Words like *soul, soul mate, karma,* and *reincarnation* have all adopted new meanings. I call this an oxymoron, like saying, "Two plus two equals five." It does not equal five, never has, but the new math, called the common core, creates a new way of thinking that changes that logic and makes two plus two equal five. My grandchildren and I have had deep conflicting conversations about this even when objects are put in front of them to show them that common core logic is not, in fact, correct.

In the pages of this book, I will give you the true meaning of these words, not the common core or New Age meaning, and show where they are placed in the circle of life. When you awaken and discover this journey, your life will change. It makes your life better by helping you become more alive and connected, giving you more control of your present life and your journey home. This is important as our children are awakening us to the realization of who we are.

If generations keep changing these meanings, they will get lost in communal thinking. With the technology age, where Google and Wikipedia have become the main sources of information, true meaning gets lost in mainstream and communal thought. Let us look at Google Dictionary's definition of a soul mate: "a person ideally suited to another as a close friend or romantic partner." This is not the true meaning of a soul mate. A soul mate is part of your karmic journey and can be an enemy, a sister, a brother, or just someone who passes through your life quickly as well. When their karmic journey is completed, they separate from you and move on. There can be this feeling that you have known them before, essentially because you have, but they are very rarely your lifelong romantic partner. With the mainstream definition, we miss out on the karmic lesson and are misguided, lost, and confused and sometimes stuck because the mainstream definition keeps changing. This book takes you back to the true meaning, going deeper, showing people who are lost in such mainstream definitions the connection and journey as it lifts the fog to reveal the journey home. You will discover that each person has an individual path, a life force and purpose that connects us all through the lifetimes.

The information in this book and my personal experiences will awaken your mind to see your own journey from life's beginning. It will make your life more exciting when a new human soul is born and help with the journey of the soul when our loved one's journey of putting things in perspective gives life on earth a purpose. You will be prepared to recognize, acknowledge, and guide the sensitive ones/empathic children when they reach out and talk about "when they were big," reminding you, "You made my body. My soul chose it."

Growing up in foster care, moving from home to home, never being mainstreamed, I was able to be led by my soul through life. I was able to experience life in a different way than most people. This helped me evolve and grow while keeping my soul free and not grounding it with dogma so I could not see my path. It is important to understand that when we mess with a child's birth, we risk interfering with the spiritual plan of that child as well as their growth and purpose in life. The child could also be removed from the family tree and bloodline for future lives. As I got older and had children of my own, I was able to recognize the early signs of a reincarnated soul. My own experiences have allowed me to see the beginning and ending of one's journey and back home again. I know that life is not just living and dying; it is a journey of many lifetimes. I understand that "[when] the soul goes through the birth process, the souls on the other side weep, while those on Earth rejoice. When the soul goes through the death process, the families on earth mourn, while those on the other side rejoice"—the journey home, the circle of life.

Three of the stories in this book, I was fortunate enough to experience from the beginning of life. It changed my life, being able to receive such validation in my work and have it be so personal. If I had been mainstreamed or not been awakened, I would have missed the signs. So as you read this book, I encourage you to open your mind, let go of mainstream thinking, and expand your ideals to other possibilities and perspectives. It is my belief that people want to find a way to connect again and find that common love and understanding. They do not know how to do this without compromising or abandoning their religious beliefs. There are many things that divide us as a human race and so many distractions that keep us from opening our eyes to the bigger picture. We just accept things without question while the signs and answers are being written off as not valid and ignored or the definition changes, making the answers unnoticeable and harder to find. If we look with clear eyes, it is all right there for us to see, and if we take a deeper look, we would see that we are all connected; the names and definitions have just changed.

As you read this book, I challenge you to let go and open yourself up so you can connect to your soul and see your purpose, realizing that the universal purpose is love. Connecting and knowing makes our life here on Earth better, more meaningful, and much easier to live. Our journey creates a story. Each life and passing becomes more exciting and conducive to bonding. In this book, I will repeat some things like "Listen to your children" to truly get that message across. We are the students and our children the teachers. Let the children pull off our masks, show us the beauty that is within, and invite us to a human existence that is sleeping within our souls.

Awaken the soul, connect the dots, and see the story as you evolve to the source.

ACKNOWLEDGMENTS

I HAVE BEEN INVESTIGATING reincarnation since 1992. My interest was ignited by my work with the paranormal and my lifetime ability to hear, speak to, and see spirits. The information I had received from the other side piqued a curiosity in me that burned in me and created a list of questions that this non-mainstreamed free thinker had to explore to find all the pieces to this large puzzle we call life.

My story begins in my first book, *Through the Cracks: The Magic in Me*, and continues in *Faded: The Circle of Life to the Soul*. This is expected to be the last book in the Awakening series, although I never know what I am going to write until it is time to write the book. I hope that you are on your way to connect your dots and that you have awakened to your true purpose, which is love. I hope that your awakening gives you a truly inspired life and that you share it with others to help heal the world.

I would like to dedicate this book to Raven Rose, Thunder Bear, and Phoenix White Owl. Without you, this book would not be possible. You are the teachers who will open the eyes of the next generation's masters to bring together and connect all to the mind, body, and soul and the universal consciousness that will awaken them to true enlightenment. You are our children, and we cannot help but notice.

Thank you. Namaste.

*The power of intuitive understanding will protect
you from harm until the end of your days.*

— Lao Tzu, 600 B.C.

INTRODUCTION

WITH THE MASS diversity of perspectives in the world today, each generation brings new ideas and explanations of how life is to be lived. Old beliefs and ways of thinking are falling to the wayside, and new thinkers are on the rise. We call this evolving.

The one thing I have recognized in this world today as this new shift is being born is that there is more of a mix that has opened their minds to new ideas and new ways of thinking.

In the rise of the millennium, a new age was born. Old beliefs that were mainly structured on religion have now started to step outside of that box and look at other perspectives. Free thinkers and critical thinking emerged from their hidden places. Free thinkers began to openly form new ideas and opinions and brought them out into the open rather than accept the old ways. A bigger picture has been acknowledged, all life has been expanded, and purpose has been added to the mix. This new change has opened new doors to sciences and discoveries and has merged them to create the new reality for all humans to create the reality they choose. The past, present, and future have evolved into one soul. This has always existed—for this is life—but has been left hidden beneath dogma, religion, and culture.

Generation Z was born into an economy that needed the support of a two-parent income, giving less time for religious teachings and culture. The family structure was changing. These children were brought outside the strict family home and experienced more of the outside world at a younger age. Their reliance on their parents was less than that of the millennials.

Gen Z grew to be more self-confident, independent, and autonomous. Technology was on the rise, and as Gen Z rose to adulthood in 2016, by 2020, they will account for one-third of the U.S. population, and they will leave behind the baby boomers' and millennials' religious dominance and influence. Their openness toward spirituality through cosmology has opened the world to new ideas and a new way of thinking. They started asking questions more openly. The internet and social media apps were introduced at a young age, where they found the answers and even more questions that moved them forward with a liberal attitude and the discovery of new trends with an abundance of social media outlets. The world became bigger, and there was a vast openness that was appealing and filled their minds. Their teachers became universal. The soul emerged, and the consciousness was discovered in a new perspective. According to a report from the Barna Group on Gen Z, "[they] are more likely to identify as atheists and agnostics, and church attendance is unimportant."

Gen Z became known as the more openly eclectic generation, creating their own spirituality from elements of various religions and spiritual traditions. Some still maintained a normal cultural affiliation to religion but did not go to church services, choosing to hold on to family beliefs embedded in past family culture by celebrating holidays.

Through these times, we have seen a mix of interpretation of religious doctrine, such as the Bible. Different groups of people from the same religious groups have different meanings for the same teachings. With both parents in the work force and the structure of the church falling because of life changes and mistrust in the church leaders themselves, this opened the door for this generation to ask new questions and find their answers outside of this religious box.

This generation—being so diverse and on the track to be the most well-educated generation, more so than their predecessors—began the shift from an organized religion, where the belief is necessary for the society to function, to a more universal and spiritual society that looks within for the answers about God and began to educate themselves on the circle of life, consciousness, and the inner soul, edging "God" out of control and adding free will. They bring to the surface more of the tools that science has provided. They are the beginning of the new age of enlightenment; they bring in new questions and want the answers to them. They want to know if God exists, and if he does, why does the belief in him come with so much control and judgment, hypocrisy and intolerance? What kind of God would allow so much death by violent acts and violence and judgment by his followers? For the true followers who give themselves truly to God, why have their lives not changed? Why is this world, which was founded by God and ruled by God, controlled by judgment, hypocrisy, discrimination, hatred, and violence? This generation does not just ask, "Does God exist?" and accept the answer "Yes" because religion says so. They want to know about the soul and the universal connection. They want to know about reincarnation and "why I look and act the way I do." They do not want to play by the rules if there are no answers as to why these are the rules. It is not because God said so anymore because who is God?

The result is the universal thought "I can get what I want with the right intention." Intention is not just want. Sending prayers and sending energy with the right intentions are the same. Doing either with the wrong intentions is also the same.

As Gen Z is capping off, a new generation is being born and making their entrance into this world. In 2010, Generation Alpha (coined and researched by sociologist Mark McCrindle) came into this world at a rate of 2.5 million births a week. At the end of 2019, they turned ten years old. They will be the first generation who will see the twenty-second century. They were shaped fully in the twenty-first century and will start (and are starting) a whole new nomenclature and are redefining new meanings. Life and God have broader meanings to them and go way beyond religious text. They are breaking free of boundaries, continuing the ways of the previous generation, and coming in with those answers that the previous generation were seeking.

Generation Alpha is living up to the vibration of their generation title. They are truly the Alpha. Technology is now a way of life. This generation does not just use technology; they also integrate it flawlessly. Social media networks such as Facebook will become a thing of the past as they make way for more innovated ideas. They are more reliant on instant information and answers that are just a click away. They strive to live in the now. They have been brought up to focus on equality and have lived with diversity where marriage is a piece of paper, where love is love, and where biracial couples are the norm and accepted. Many of this generation have been raised by single parents. Living in the fast lane has made mainstreaming harder to do with this generation, and they eschew organized religion. Right out of the womb, these children have always known who they are, and they are movers and shakers. Old prophecies have been fulfilled, and the shift has come full circle with this generation. They surely hold true to their generation title; they are the Alphas.

As I encounter and interact with this generation, I find that many are older souls. They know who they were in the last incarnation, know what they are capable of to achieve their purpose, and are ready to awaken the unenlightened. In my last book, *Faded: The Circle of Life to the Soul*, I talked about the soul's rebirth and our pre-birth planning in the life between lives—the life that the soul experiences between the life it had before incarnation and the life before the soul reincarnates on its next journey—and how it all connects to the circle of life as we journey through lifetimes with a new body and the same soul, with each journey bringing in a new purpose. The Alpha generation are less mainstreamed and are holding onto their "life between lives" memory and the natural gifts they come into this world with. As infants, they seem more determined to start their new journey and develop and advance more quickly. They come in like firecrackers and do not stop. Henry Rose Lee, international speaker and author, describes Alphas as "millennials on steroids." Parents are noticing as these children are seeing other souls still not reborn and seeing the true soul identities of others of their generation, feeling their vibrations, and showing their spiritual gifts. They are communicating at younger ages and recognizing those whom they knew in previous lifetimes, alerting their chosen parents of this lifetime to ask the question "What is happening to my child?" and seek out help from those who have this knowledge, questioning their own religious beliefs in being able to clearly give them answers as their children say, "Mommy, when I was big . . . before my journey here."

This generation are being born with a higher vibration and are holding onto their memories from their previous journeys as souls. They are deeply connected to the universal consciousness and fully aware of this connection. They hold onto the abilities each soul holds within their soul consciousness.

For generations, as we evolve, humans have been becoming more and more disenchanted and held back from their own souls' journeys, not paying attention to signs or messages that their consciousness has been giving them because of old standards and judgments. New generations reject conformity and evolve, making an impact and making others take notice of things that have been brushed aside for centuries.

In 1997, at around the age of seventy-seven, Dr. Ian Stevenson published his 2,268-page, two-volume work called *Reincarnation and Biology* and, shortly after, a condensed version, *Where Reincarnation and Biology Intersect*. These books show his research on children's memories of previous lives. Stevenson collected data and evidence from thousands of children who remembered their past lives spontaneously. After extensive research and interviews, he looked to identify the deceased person who matched the child's memory. He did not just stop there; he took his research further and verified the memory by matching the deceased life, birthmarks, birth defects, and scars, many being verified through medical records and living families. Stevenson's system was designed to rule out, one by one, all possible normal explanations of the child's memory. He took an interest in the behavior of the children, identifying and linking them to the past life memories the children remembered.

Stevenson opened the doors for others to pursue his life-shifting research. Much of his research was done outside of the United States, in areas such as Asia, India, Sri Lanka, Thailand, Lebanon, Turkey, Burma, West Africa, and tribes of the Pacific Northwest. He found these countries easier to find cases. These countries and their cultures were more open and receptive to the concept of reincarnation and were more willing to speak openly about their belief in reincarnation and the memories they held with extensive detail. In the United States, reincarnation is recognized as taboo within much of the Americans' religious and culture sects at that time because of their culture or religious beliefs; they feel that it is a sin to recognize reincarnation as real except in terms of their religious icon. However, with the United

States being a melting pot and with the rise of New Age thinkers and spirituality, Stevenson was able to research over a thousand cases in the United States alone. His research was incredibly detailed and thorough when investigating the past lives of children, and never would he accept third-party information; he only accepted the information from the person who had witnessed the action or the child spoken to. His research included an eighty-page registration form that asked for various details of the case. When all evidence was obtained—photos, notes, and interviews—they would be coded and filed in a database.

Dr. Ian Stevenson and his team of colleagues who followed in his footsteps and carried on his investigations with a firm belief in his studies believed that "[these subjects should not be studied scientifically since it is so far removed from usual empirical areas of investigation . . . These cases are not about proof; it is about evidence." All his research is documented and filed at the University Of Virginia, where he founded and directed the Division of Perpetual Studies, which investigates the paranormal. His research is on reincarnation in children and that the idea of emotions, memories, and physical bodily features can be transferred from one lifetime to the next. He later helped found the Society for Scientific Exploration. After his death in 2007 at the age of eighty-eight, other researchers came to the forefront, continued his work, and wrote about them—namely, Jim B. Tucker, who continued his work after Ian's death, along with other researchers, Tom Shroder, Carol Bowman, and Dr. Brian Weis.

This book is supportive of this work as well as my experiences and real stories from past lives and between life regressions. I present to you the stories of children whom I have encountered who have memories of their previous lives as well as my experience in working with this next generation, Generation Alpha, who have come to awaken a sleeping, disenchanted world with their stories of other lives and worlds and how they will impact our human lives. Through my life, I had never meant to be a teacher of death and rebirth, to be a free thinker and one who has been in search for the truth and my own spirituality. The answers led me here and opened me up to see with open eyes death and rebirth. The signs are there, and the truth lies in the reincarnated souls, so for those of you who have heard those words—"Mommy, when I was big"—listen as they tell you their journey back to Earth . . .

This book does not stop there, for "Mommy, when I was big" is only the beginning as they grow to be our sensitive ones who prove to be the vital opening for humanity, teaching us to grow into more heart-centered human beings and awaken all to the intuitive awareness that we hold deep within our soul. They want to instill kindness and compassion and show us that we all have one path in life, and that is one of love.

These sensitive ones come with struggles as they are born into a world that is filled with dogma and judgment and as they try and bring sunshine to the darkness and understanding to the confused and turn hope into belief. They show us that faith is universal and that being connected with intention brings us together as one. These sensitive ones are misunderstood and, through the beliefs of the past, have been labeled, medicated, and shut down. They are the new beginning. They are the opportunity for change. They show us who we are, the answers to our questions. They lead us to our soul consciousness, which has been hidden and of which we have been unaware, and to help us discover our own individuality and intuitiveness.

Let them show you who you are and listen to the children when they say, "Mommy, when I was big," for it is only the beginning to shine the light on our powerful, sensitive ones who will open our eyes and bring us back to love.

THE LINK

Is each raindrop like a life and each cloud the overall essence of the soul?

IT ALL BEGINS WITH THE SOUL

Everything the body experiences is recorded in the soul

THE SOUL IS consciousness that fills the body and becomes the true essence and energy of who we are. When the soul fills the body at birth, it gives our body and the human being that we are to become life. We need both the body and the soul to have human life. The soul then becomes our connection to our humanness, the non-physical essence of all living beings.

Each soul is unique to itself, holding its own identity and vibrational energy. The soul appears as an energy of light, contains its own personality and intelligence, and functions as vibrational waves that have no limitations.

When the soul gives life to a body upon entering it at birth, it has no gender. The soul is genderless; it has the vibrational energy of both the male and the female. The body gives the soul its gender. The soul contains both male and female energies that come together at birth as one. Humans give birth to the body; the soul chooses the life and the body to experience the lesson.

Our soul remains the same energy as previous lifetimes and uses the body as its vehicle to manifest itself here on the earthly plane. The soul carries this energy through each incarnation and carries the memory of each lifetime, with the lessons learned and experienced. This journey is an in-depth look at the learning experiences a soul requires mentally and spiritually through all lifetimes. The soul will always attract toward itself what it needs to learn in each lifetime. Those lessons and experiences are looked at to see how those experiences have developed into our current spiritual evolution and to help us connect, in the next incarnation, to our humanness.

The soul evolves in an accelerated way by returning to Earth. Prior to the soul's return, it has agreed to be put in a situation on Earth and have a three-dimensional experience that will allow it to react. How it will react will determine how quickly it will ascend. Your soul's path has brought you to this lifetime, to where you are today. For a soul to ascend to another journey, it must incarnate into a material form and find its vehicle, a body where one forms a connection with their human self and they become an unlimited being living in an earthly, limited world. On this three-dimensional journey, one of the main goals we need to achieve is to transform all our emotions of fear, resentment, and jealousy to evolve in the next journey. These emotions become underlying patterns that keep getting played out in each lifetime as we look for an explanation to our problem, karma, or unfinished business from previous lives. If it is not resolved in one life, it continues in the next life.

The circle of life travels to the soul, and when separated from the body, the spirit becomes the vessel for the soul. The one organ that stays connected to the soul even after death is the heart. Even when the heart stops beating, there is a transition of energy that comes from the heart to the soul and then to the spirit. It holds our love connection that is carried in the spirit and soul.

The endocrine gland is where the soul finds its avenue of expression and equates energy through our spirit centers, called chakras. The soul fills in the dimensional space and energy within the heart chakra and will be released upon death. Energy such as the soul can only be transformed and never destroyed. Our soul is weightless until it enters the physical body. Our soul is infinite. When the soul makes the decision to return to Earth, at the beginning of that lifetime, the soul sets out to expand its awareness. The soul carries with it a knowing and consciousness that will direct you to the situations and people in the scenarios that need to be corrected. It is important to remember that your child chose you to help them achieve their goals and learn their lessons as they help you remember and achieve yours. Noticing and recognizing what your child is saying and doing can help you answer the "What is my lesson?" question that most people have. Everything you are—your personality, beliefs, aspiration, talents, and fears—is a result of your soul's many incarnations. At the early stages of an incarnation, including birth, there are many signs of their life here on Earth. Their past life will identify things such as unfinished business and karmic debt. You can also identify patterns and fears from a traumatic death in a past life that will and can cause issues in this lifetime. When the issues that are present from a child's past life are resolved, their present lives can be happier and more fulfilling. The benefit of recognizing past-life stories in young children is to heal wounds and finish what needs to be finished early in life if possible. Your child will challenge you to step outside your box, become more connected, and explore new perspectives. Most of all, you will be able to connect and form a closeness with your child.

Have you ever taken notice of a newborn baby when it notices its earthly life for the first time? As months go by and the baby grows and struggles to gain control of their body, they seem like they know what to do; they just cannot control their body. Soon, their soul connects to their new body, and they begin to gain control of the body's functions. When my own children were babies, I did not have all the knowledge as I do now, so I did not recognize this when they were babies and their souls were expanding into their new bodies. When my children grew up and had children of their own and I was blessed with grandchildren, I started to see, understand, and verify the birth process and the soul's journey. Before I could see and understand this process, I had to become mindful, let go of my ego, allow myself to be open, and be humble and a student who questions the present norm. What is normal anyway? To me, I am normal. Although my belief system was not mainstream, I still needed to expand outside my circle. It was not as hard for me as it has been for mainstream believers. My childhood helped me with that, although I never thought that I was here to be ruled. I had a sense that this body and this place had their reasons, that free will is not just a physical law but also a universal law. Free will encompasses the spirit and includes the soul. The soul having free will—is that possible? You mean it is just not this nothingness, this ghostly mist that comes out of the body when you die?

I have always found it odd that humans believe in the ghosts of their loved ones—communicating and comforting while protecting us from harm and giving us advice—but when you use words like *soul consciousness, reincarnation, life between lives,* or even *astral travel,* they shake their heads and say, "No way. There is no proof that that happens, and I will not believe it until there is scientific proof of such things or the Bible tells me so." This concept kind of sounds contradicting to me.

My belief is that we miss out on so many experiences by limiting ourselves to restrictive thoughts or mainstream thinking. Our mainstream thinking tells us that children, when born, are newly on this earth and have nothing but what this life is going to teach them and to fill their human lives with. What we do not seem to think is that the newborn has a vast amount of knowledge held in his or her soul consciousness from many lifetimes. They may even hold messages from our passed loved ones, and they may see them, when we cannot, standing right in front of us. They know what heaven looks like and sounds like. They remember why they are here and who they are. They have all the abilities and answers that most are seeking as adults. The problem is that most of us miss out on this information because we are blinded by our belief system. This spiritual little being becomes our mainstreamed little human whom we bring up and mold by the book. When they say or do things that seem out of the ordinary, we ignore and dismiss them and then cover them up with mainstream explanations that satisfy us. We laugh off things like "Mommy, when I was big," "Mommy, when I was a girl, your mother," or "I want to go to see my other mommy." We ignore signs like the cries and fears of our child when meeting someone for the first time or their immediate attachment to certain people for no reason. We see our child as only a physical bundle of joy, not as a spiritual being who brings with him or her many lifetimes and new beginnings, who has a soul consciousness, whose five senses are expanded and extra sensitive, and whose free will is more than physical. One of these natural abilities is the ability to astral-travel when they sleep.

Children and Astral Traveling

Having always been able to astral-travel proved to me that this body has a soul. I was only a toddler when I was able to astral-travel outside of the closet I was locked in on a nightly basis. That ability kept me from panic and any real trauma that a toddler could endure from being in a small confined, dark area for long periods. I just needed to discover more about the body–soul connection and spent many years researching and asking those who had viable knowledge. I was able to apply that research and knowledge and prove to myself more things about children and their souls' connections to their bodies.

When my son was about three years old, give or take a few (the same age I was), I often wondered why in the morning, he knew what was going on or what was on TV the night before when he was fast asleep in his crib until one night, when I had my grandson in the living room, trying to get him to sleep. He had a few days of long car rides to and from Connecticut, visiting family, and had had much sleep, and tonight was the night he was now wide awake. Since I was the home mom and grandma, I was the one staying up with this very active little guy.

It was just past midnight; my son had been sleeping for over four hours now.

My grandson, wide-eyed, suddenly started waving, saying, "Bye-bye, Dee," as his eyes followed something going to my son's room.

I got up, grandson in my arms, and went to my son's room, where this light mist was slowly being absorbed into my son's sleeping little body. I went over to the crib and lightly touched him; he was chilly, so I placed the blanket over his arms and whispered good night.

My grandson said, "Shhh. Nanny, Dee sleeping."

I hugged him and smiled, and we left the room.

Now some of you are now totally mortified because your religious beliefs would have sent you down a totally different road. I assure you that no possessions were happening. He was astral-traveling. Astral traveling is when one's soul is separated from one's physical body for the purpose of traveling to places. My son's soul was within our little apartment, or maybe he was visiting loved ones on the other side or his soul family. When my grandson asked, I just told him he was a little angel at work in his sleep. I would also like to add for your comfort and knowledge that this is common in children and very natural until they are mainstreamed between the ages of five and nine. I like to refer to this mainstreaming as human grounding.

For the rest of that evening, I put my grandson to sleep and did some research to verify what my thoughts were on what had taken place. I had some knowledge but not enough for this mama. I wanted to see the big picture. I needed to process this. I decided the next night that I would put my son down to sleep like I had done every night since his birth and, when he fell asleep, go sit in the rocking chair in his room and see what, if anything, I could see. Since I had seen his soul returning, maybe I could see it at the beginning of his travels. Well, needless to say, that first night, I managed to rock myself to sleep, but I was able to see the trip back as I had done the night before. I also did the same thing I had done the night before and waited for him to return fully. Then I went to his crib and touched him. His body once again felt cool, so I covered him up, whispered good night, and went off to bed myself.

The next few days, I did some more research on astral travel and sleep. Now being a natural at astral travel, I never actually went so far as to research how I did it until I got older because it was so natural, I thought it was just something humans did, and I was never told differently. This journey usually occurs during sleep, although it can be done during deep meditation. Astral traveling, unlike dreaming, is a tangible experience and is not simply an image occurring in your mind. One's astral experience is solely one's own journey. Astral travel is also referred to as an out-of-body experience (OBE), where the soul, subtle body detaches from the physical body. This is not a dream or a hallucination. It is not psychological; it is a tangible experience. Many of these experiences happen without knowledge or practice while in deep sleep. With children who have not experienced human grounding, it just happens when the body is at rest and in REM sleep.

There are four stages of sleep, and in each stage, the brain waves progressively get larger and slower, while sleep gets deeper. The four stages are awake, non-REM 1, non-REM 2, and REM—also known as beta waves, alpha waves, theta waves, and delta waves, respectively. Brain waves are responsible for everything we think, feel, perceive, and do. Astral travel and past-life regression occur in the slower brain waves of our body–soul connection. To understand this process, it is helpful to understand the different brain wave sleep patterns:

Beta — These daytime brain waves dominate in normal wakeful states and when you are deeply focused, such as when you are focused on a cognitive task, trying to solve a problem, or making important decisions.

Alpha — Alpha waves are involved in how we think, feel, communicate, sleep, and generally function. Alpha brain waves are active while you are resting, especially when your eyes are closed and right before you drift off to sleep.

Theta — These occur during sleep and have been observed in very deep states of meditation. This is known as the realm of the subconscious. This stage is only experienced briefly as you drift off to sleep. The theta state is exceedingly difficult to experience through conscious effort. You enter this state in that moment just before you enter deep sleep, where you're neither awake nor passed out. Theta waves are between 3 Hz and 7 Hz.

Delta — This refers to slow-wave sleep and aids in characterizing the depth of sleep. Delta brain waves are associated with the deepest levels of sleep, relaxation, and peace of mind. Here is where lucid dreaming begins, past-life (between current life and future life) regression therapy takes place, and astral travel happens. At this level, there is no awareness of the physical body's needs. Some people have the ability to remember conversations in the room and things that went on when they awaken.

Eye movements are rapid where the eyes move from side to side and the brain waves are more active. While the soul is out of the body and the physical body is still, it is hard to wake the person. Awakening can occur more easily after being startled abruptly but leaves the person disoriented. When in the state of astral traveling, the body does not move. When the person gets startled awake, the soul returns quickly to the body, and the person jumps awake. When the soul leaves the body to astral-travel and is in a state of stillness, this is what is known to many as sleep paralysis.

Sleep paralysis happens when the soul is about to switch from the physical plane to the astral plane and is one of the signs of astral travel. This is a state where your mind is conscious and your body is asleep. Your body feels like it is pinned down, and you cannot move your limbs. This is frightening for our human self, young and old. Even newborns can experience sleep paralysis, and many times, this is misdiagnosed as night terrors. Newborns only have a past life and an in-between life to reference, and this triggers fear for night terrors, such as the way they are being diagnosed. I always tell my clients who come to me with this to always be mothers first—check all concerned issues, like breathing, and if you feel more comfortable, check with your doctor. If the medical diagnosis is night terrors or if there is no medical reason, this is what is happening. The infant is not grounded completely to the body, and it likes to travel when it is in the delta state or REM sleep. Just pick your baby up and cuddle and soothe them. A young child or an infant does this naturally, whereas someone who is human grounded must deliberately attempt to control their brain activity to achieve this altered level of consciousness. This, in either level of humanness, is in no way dangerous and, in both cases, a natural process.

Breathing changes are another sign. Heavy breathing is a sign that you are completely relaxed but need to calm yourself to a slower rhythm of breathing. So when you are having sleep paralysis and you feel like you cannot breathe, it is not because some entity is smothering you or trying to possess you; it is because your breathing slows down in this state. The normal reflex is to gasp when you startle yourself to awaken from this switch. The fear of this state is the lack of knowing or understanding the process. This is more prominent in young children because of their natural ability to astral-travel before human grounding.

The feeling of flying, floating, or weightlessness is prominent. Your heart rate increases. The heart works fast to boost the blood flow to your body parts because the switch is not easy on your body after human grounding. You hear a vibrational sound because of the energy shift, and it increases when you are ready to enter the astral plane. At this point, you will start to hear the voices of the spiritual world. The sleeping body, in its stillness, is cool to the touch. I have personally never felt any physical temperature changes while astral-traveling because it is my soul that is traveling, not my physical body. When I had touched my son's body, his body, both times, felt cool.

Vibrational tingling (before exit) and vigorous vibrations occur, and they can feel like physical sensations. Loud humming or buzzing sounds occur simultaneously with the vibrations and voices from the astral plane. I have noticed with my little ones that listening to meditation music such as Tibetan bowls or Gregorian chants has soothed them. The vibration of the bowls excites them, like they remember the feeling and must touch them. I personally have nine bowls myself, all different tones, and my little ones love playing with them. It is fun watching them learn how to strike them to get the proper tone. I let them pick which tone they like, show them how it is done, watch them try and do it themselves, and see how excited they get when they do it right. Another sign is the feeling of pressure to the head, from the brow center to the crown center, like a band being tightened around your head. The astral body does not lose its connection to the physical body.

All these signs, I give to you so that when your child talks to you about their journey and mentions some of these signs, you do not automatically go into a panic. You will have a slight understanding that they are going through a natural process of astral traveling.

Children's sleep patterns are a little different by age. Children up to three years of age go through the sleep cycle in sixty minutes. At the age of five, they have grown to the adult length of ninety minutes. Adults cycle through the various stages of sleep. Babies are evenly divided between REM and non-REM, each stage lasting only fifty minutes for the first nine months of life. When a child has this astral journey, they are allowing their consciousness to travel through solid objects and exit from the body. If, at any point, fear becomes relevant, the journey will end.

For many years after the incident with my grandson and the first discovery of my son's astral traveling, I would go in his room and sit and watch. This, of course, was much easier for me to see because of my abilities and the fact that I was not mainstreamed; my own experiences were my guide. I do find that mainstreaming your child—telling your child that he or she is making up stories, ignoring them, or turning to mainstream religion to find answers instead of stepping outside the religious structure to find a source of information that is credible—is truly not the best way to find the truth. You would not go to a dictionary to find a recipe for cupcakes, would you? You are not going to find answers in a place that is not open to the concept and closes its beliefs off to ideas outside their perspective. Finding the right information and being knowledgeable about the experiences of your child is an immense catalyst for their personal and spiritual development. Some children's stories are part of their wonderful, spirited imagination, which is just as wonderful and important for the child's development, but there are those stories that connect them to a life lived before or adventures they have gone on while sleeping. It is known that children start developing a vivid imagination at around three years of age when they play with dolls, stuffed animals, and other toys. This could also signal stories of past lives. Listen and think in an age-appropriate manner when determining between imagination and past lives.

Things that kids may say at a young age when they have had an experience include the following: "Mommy, last night, I went flying"; "Mommy, I saw you crying, but I could not come to you because I disappeared"; and "Mommy, I went up, and then I came down." When your child says things like these or similar things, do not freak out or run to your religious organization and ask for a cleansing because some evil entity is coming after your child. Just listen and talk to them. Journal what he or she is talking about and research or contact one of the many people who are open and knowledgeable about what is happening. It is important to keep an open mind.

When my son had just turned fourteen years old, shortly after his coming-of-age/rite-of-passage ceremony, his uncle, who was his best friend and godfather, was killed in a motorcycle accident. My son was understandably devastated, and it took much strength for us to get through this tragedy. A parent's heart breaks even more when their own child is feeling pain that they cannot put a bandage on. We lose sleep over this, as I did. Again, I was back to sitting in his room and watching him as he slept. He would wake up in the middle of the night in distress, and my room was at the end of the hallway. I wanted to be there to ease him back to sleep. Yes, I know he was fourteen, but dealing with the loss of someone so close can cause more emotional issues that can be damaging at any age. I was always open with my beliefs about death and my spirituality and had taught my children the same. That in itself helped get him through this tragic part of his life. It was imperative to talk to my son about death, and I never believed in sugarcoating. When he was a baby and learning how to talk, I did not baby-talk him. I talked to him like I would anyone else, and he learned to understand even when he could not speak.

One night, as I was sitting there, drinking my nighttime tea and watching my son, I saw this orb-like mist come to my son, and two just flew away.

As they were leaving, I said out loud, "Just bring him back."

I waited for what seemed to be a long time, but soon enough, the orb mists were back. Two came in; one filled my son, and the other one disappeared.

I whispered, "Thank you," got up, checked on my son, and went down the hall to bed like I did when he was a baby.

In the morning, when my son got up, he seemed different, happier, like the darkness had lifted. He ate his breakfast and grabbed his backpack, and as he left for school, he turned and said to me, "Mom, Uncle David is okay. He came to me last night, and we went flying. He told me he would be watching me grow into a man and for me to be the best I can be. He loves me, and he will be okay. He said I would see him again."

After that night, the darkness was gone, and he honored the memory of his uncle, sometimes with tears and heartache, but now I would pass his room and hear him talking to his uncle. He remembered astral-traveling and was able to describe the experience. When I asked him if he was afraid when he was traveling, he said to me that when he realized what he was doing, because of the teachings from his upbringing, he felt comfortable and not afraid, and he was able to validate his experience.

Your children are not broken.
They are simply differently abled.

— Meg Blackburn Lousy, MSC, PHD

OUTSIDE THE BOX

Listen to your children. Hear them. You never know what wonder and magic they can share with us. Love them with all your might, listen to them with all that you are, and know that sometimes it just requires a different set of ears to really hear them. You will find those in your heart.

— Meg Blackburn Lousy, MSC, PHD

YES, HE/SHE IS probably talking to and seeing Grandpa, and yes, he/she may have an invisible friend. It could be his/her guardian angel or even part of his/her soul family to help them adjust in their new human life. I believe that was how I had survived my childhood.

Your child's gifts may seem unique, like he or she was born special, but we are all born with these same gifts and more and still have them within us. Young children just have not been completely human grounded yet. As soon as they grow and go to school, it will fade unless you nurture it from the start. Their memories are pushed back into their subconscious and will take much more effort to retrieve.

Mainstreaming and human grounding are tough to avoid because with emphasis on being politically correct and having firm opinions on what is right and wrong, it is hard not to be mainstreamed and human grounded. I do understand, and it has been a fact that most people become victims of nervous tension and anxiety, of just the prospect of death and the thought that our own children have memories of lives other than this life that we as parents have given them. That can be scary, especially with all the talk and beliefs about possessions that penetrate some religious beliefs. Do your best to not get wrapped up in this prospect or lose sleep and overthink this. I personally am not one who subscribes to the belief in demons. I believe that we create our own dark energy through negativity, emotion, and anger. In all my years of being the soul that I am and having the abilities I have, I have never encountered a "demon," and I would be one of the first people they would go after if they were real. So take a deep breath and, without provoking them, listen to your child. Look outside the box and pay attention; you may be witnessing something life changing. Our human consciousness gives us an indication that the soul carries with it a personality and that it exists not only here, on the earthly plane, but also in the in-between and pre-birth as well as in the past life.

CHILDREN REMEMBERING THE PAST

MANY CHILDREN I have talked to remember what it was like in the womb and speak of being in the womb and traveling down the birth canal and the birthing process. For some, that memory is so profound that even as adults, they can still remember coming into this plane. I work with clients who wish to be regressed and go through the birth canal and back into the womb as a way back into a past life. That regression has had great success. (My research on this technique is credited to Dr. Brian Weiss, MD.)

Children do not need regression if they have not been human grounded; their vibrations are still extremely high. Parents' concern tends to rise at the thought that young children remembering and expressing their past-life memories may not have the maturity level to understand or may feel differently about such memories, making them feel like outcasts, resulting in the inability to make friends or the tendency to become subject to bullying. This is surely a natural concern for parents to have about their children's mental and emotional health. In all my cases, I have never known this to be true; nor have I read a case as such. I do not believe in this outcome, and my reasoning for this is because the soul consciousness carries these memories. These memories are carried from lifetime to lifetime. When the child remembers and voices these memories, there is no feeling of being different because this is who they are and have always been. This is who they know and who they were when born into this world. They have nothing to compare it with; they know nothing different. The worldview for them has not been established, and "right or wrong" has not been completely embedded into them yet. They are at another level where their reality is more attuned and still attached to the other worlds. There have been cases where the child's memory is so extensive and remarkably detailed that the child insists on returning to visit the place or family they remember from a previous life. Making that contact has brought amazing healing.

Even in these cases, there have not been any documented emotional or mental issues because of the remembering of past lives. Children are very enthusiastic in the telling of their stories, so much so that many parents feel that these stories are products of an overactive imagination.

One day, visiting the doctor's office for a scheduled appointment, Linda, because of not having someone to watch her son, took him with her. Her son ran straight to the playroom to play with many of the toys that were in the children's playroom. There were no other kids there, so Lucas, Linda's son, played by himself. The doctor's office was packed, so the wait was longer than usual. After a while, two other mothers with little boys around the same age as Lucas, who was three, visited the office. Lucas happened to look up to see both these little boys wave with excitement at each other. The two boys ran to Lucas, and these three little strangers embraced one another like they had known one another. That moment did seem a little odd for Linda and the two other parents, but they just cooed it away, relishing in the sweet, loving moment they had just witnessed of their little boys. They played together like they were old friends. A few minutes later, they started talking about memories of time spent together.

One would say, "'Member when we did this?" and they would laugh and agree.

They talked back and forth like they were old friends getting lost in the memories of the past for about five minutes. Then Linda got called for her appointment, and the boys exchanged goodbyes.

"Bye, David. Bye, Tommy. Bye, Gary," they said as Lucas left with his mother.

Who were David, Tommy, and Gary? Linda asked the two mothers what their sons' names were, and they had replied with "My son's name is Ethan" and "My son's name is Ryan." Were these boys just mimicking something each saw in their own lives? If so, who were David, Tommy, and Gary, and what were the odds of all three boys meeting in this lifetime, acting as they did toward one another, acting like old friends who had not seen one another in a long time, running into one another, and catching up on old times? Maybe they had been brothers or best friends. Could they have recognized one another's past-life identity? This was an unprovoked response from three young toddlers who displayed evidence of soul/personality recognition. No questions were asked of the boys; it all just happened naturally. In this case, no research was done to determine who David, Tommy, and Gary were. Linda was in a perplexed state of mind and did not pursue the incident with a simple follow-up question as to who Tommy, Gary, and David were right after the boys had parted ways. In such a case, we cannot claim that this was a past-life memory, but at the same time, we cannot say with certainty that it was not. We can approach this case with an attitude of wanting to learn as much about the possibilities that are present in cases such as this one. What if Linda had access to the knowledge to pursue this moment in time and the experience of her son that day, the knowledge to look outside the box?

Many conservative Christian churches teach us that seeking knowledge outside of the church's strict beliefs, such as purchasing books about reincarnation, is a sin, even if purchasing a book would be helpful to the well-being of a child. Therefore, it is safe to say that seeking a specialist in the field of past lives and reincarnation would also be considered a sin. This can lead to much stress, and the choice between the two can be very conflicting and scary, but the fact remains that it is your choice. While making that choice, it is important to know that the past-life memories that children have are very meaningful to many of the children who experience them. They feel ownership of these memories and the prior events that they have experienced. These children are often said to possess knowledge of a deceased individual that they could not have had or been able to obtain by any normal means. In most cases, these memories do not always appear to be accessible all the time. These memories, at times, can describe a particular feature about a place or even a person. These memories are part of this soul's/personality's journey, and many of these memories are said to be from near the end of a previous life, but this is not always the case. Children can also act out these memories, and sometimes they can remember more than one lifetime—as in the case of Owl Phoenix later in this book.

Fear is as natural to us humans as breathing.

FEAR —AND THE PANIC BUTTON WHAT NEXT?

WE PUT SO much stigma on spiritual phenomena, only staying within our own religious box, fearing some sort of judgment if we step outside of that box. Then we miss out on other possibilities for truth and enlightenment. Instead, we jump to judgment, allow the fear of the unknown to take over, and question the idea of whether there is something wrong with our child. We contemplate the idea of whether we need to consider medical or spiritual counsel. Of course, if you feel that there is a medical reason for your child's actions, seek advice and counsel from your medical doctor. In my opinion, putting them through some type of psychological child therapy or religious exorcism can be more damaging. If you feel that you have a need to seek out help, find someone who is certified in this field. There are many people out there who dedicate themselves in the field of past lives and who specialize in children. At the end of this book is a list of knowledgeable and respected authors who are doctors in their field to give you a verified, professional view. The main and key "musts" before seeking these specialized persons are as follows:

<u>Let Go of Fear</u> — Fear holds you back. If you do feel fear, let it be the open door to the motivator in finding the truth. Remember that there is nothing to fear about reincarnation because we have all achieved it many times. Fear is a human emotion that can alter our decision-making process. Fear blocks your soul's progress and therefore should be overcome if at all possible so that you can learn about and be open to your child's experience.

<u>Let Go of Judgment</u> — Judging the possibilities can only close your mind up to the awakening of new concepts.

<u>Let Go of Ego</u> — You do not know everything! Be a student so you can recognize what makes sense. We would all like that one piece to fit in

the puzzle, but that one side might not balance the piece for others to slide in and flow through. Give it up and look for a piece that fits even if you do not like its shape.

Open Your Mind — Opening your mind opens you up to other beliefs so that connecting the dots is possible. A closed mind blocks the flow of truth and blinds you to other possibilities.

Listen with That Open Mind — Many of the concepts that you will hear will go way beyond your own personal belief system. To truly listen will challenge those beliefs but bring you closer to the truth.

By doing all this, you will be opening a door that will change the way you look at life, death, and rebirth and bring you even closer to your child. When seeking out a specialist, it is important to respect their field and, most of all, ask questions to help you gain clarity.

*Death and life are only
separated by destiny.*

— Frances Banks

PAST LIVES

The journey and destiny of the soul link past, present, and future lives to create and help one evolve to oneness.

A S THE TRANSFORMATION of our planet intensifies and new discoveries and sciences open doors to exploring new beliefs, the exploration of past lives is realized as a great spiritual adventure. Past lives are bleeding through and coloring the lives of some unsuspecting cultures and old beliefs, and cultures are having a hard time staying true to old thoughts and doctrines. Old beliefs are mixing with new beliefs. Many blend Christian faiths with Eastern or New Age beliefs and refuse to be confined to the teachings of their churches or the guidance of their religious leaders because new generations of children, their children, are awakening them to new truths. They are learning that past lives are extensions of ourselves and are also evidence of reincarnation. To reincarnate is to have a past life, which is an amazing phenomenon and is not merely a belief; it is a remarkable fact of life. With children who remember their past lives and all the research that has been done through the years, it explains why the belief in rebirth has become so strong in the twenty-first century.

Through the years, as many have sought for the answers to this remarkable fact of life, it has become an increasing source of healing and inspiration that has made way for the rise in spirituality and true enlightenment. More and more people are on the quest for and in pursuit of a spiritual experience. Scientists examine *what is.* They eliminate all possibilities, and if, in some cases, past-life recall remains (and it is) unexplainable, they have strong evidence of an indestructible soul, which has cast suspicion on the belief that past-life memories come from the brain, a popular belief among non-believers in past lives. The denial that past lives are part of our soul consciousness and are not just memories stored in the brain becomes contradictory to certain religious doctrines.

The belief in past lives has permeated most cultures for thousands of years. There have been people in every culture who have been born with memories of past lives and proved it through the examination of the memory to be truthful and accurate. In some cultures, it is believed that an elderly person would choose and announce to a young female relative that he or she has chosen them to be reborn from, and when the child is born of the chosen one, they immediately look for signs of the deceased family member, looking for their behavior and birthmarks and listening to their words when they speak.

Dr. Ian Stevenson, through his research, found that, indeed, there are cultures that practice such beliefs. He believed that what we believe and intend before death can influence our next incarnation. It is normal for a deceased loved one to reincarnate into the same family in the next lifetime, but it could take years of earthly time to make that transition. He also believed that the spiritually adept can predict and direct their next incarnation. Some believe that immediate reincarnation is the only way to keep the flow of the journey evolving.

My belief is that the soul has more than one family circle. Each incarnation and past life adds to that circle, and when we choose to reincarnate, we can choose to do so with our spiritual past-life family from any of our lifetimes because the soul needs to choose an incarnation with the right measure of challenges and opportunities for the learning and development needed to evolve. When the lesson is learned, the soul evolves. So maybe for that chosen lesson, you need to reincarnate with a soul from three lifetimes ago. Understand that whatever it is we need to learn, many souls need many lifetimes to learn it and break patterns. Another piece of information that stirs this cauldron is that Earth is not the only planet and that humans are not the only living species. Through my time as a regression therapist, I have yet to hear stories of "Mommy, when I was a monkey," but I do keep my mind open because I do believe it is possible. There is a little thing called free will; we have it, and so does our soul.

I do challenge you to, just for one day, let go of ego and dogma, anything that keeps you grounded in your box of beliefs and judgments. Then open your eyes, listen, and observe. Look into your child's eyes and really listen to their play and the questions they ask. Are the things they are expressing something learned in this lifetime? Look at things through my eyes by changing the lens in yours because as Wayne Dyer says, "If you change the way you look at things, the things you look at change." If you need more clarity on this, look up *The Shift* on Netflix or other movie sources by Wayne Dyer. The main goal here is not to change your beliefs but to expand them and adopt a different perspective so you can evolve, understand without fear a past-life memory, and recognize it in your children at the beginning of this lifetime. Think about how that would help you understand your child and the journey he or she took to get to you, why they chose you.

Take a day to look at every living thing, noticing its essence and feeling its vibration. If you can truly let go and allow yourself to do this, your life will expand and evolve. Through the years of having children of my own and multiple grandchildren, the greatest lesson I feel I have taught them is to use their senses, to feel the energy and know what is meant for them by listening to their gut and inner higher self. My greatest tools in this have been crystals, stones, and tarot and oracle cards. Everything has an energy and vibration. Close your eyes and feel it. The one that is right for you will let you know by the pulling or tingling sensation in the palm of your hand. It is a beautiful thing to watch a child as they close their eyes and brush their palms over things to choose which is right for them. After all, they are the sensitive ones. They feel and manifest everything without fear.

Children are the most powerful when they are between their birth years and three years old because they have not been taught to fear or judge. Mainstream thought has not been imprinted in them yet. Many lessons after that age are geared toward fear. "Fear everything!" I say *know* everything. Know how it feels. Use your senses. Let go of fear and judgment. Open your mind and soul so your child can show you and teach you of the things they know—their past lives and the lessons they have learned and taken with them.

From the moment of birth, we start the learning pattern
of fear. As we form our coherent thoughts,
we are indoctrinated with fear.

— Dr. Brian Weiss

FEAR — WHAT WILL THEY SAY?

WE AS HUMANS are very grounded in our earthly lives, and most have this fearful "What will they say? What will they think?" mentality. We follow the guidelines of what people such as our religious leaders, our parents, our neighbors, or even our best friends think, afraid to go outside of the box and be different because that would not be the norm of mainstream life or what some call "politically correct."

When children start speaking of past lives and challenging our lifelong beliefs, we fear that we would be criticized and judged. We sit in fear, wondering if it is possible that there are parallel realities. "Our child is talking about another reality. Is there more than one reality, and is my child, in essence, a part of two realities?" The thought enters your mind that this is not what you were taught. "That is not what my religious leader and church-going friends believe." Then you say, "But my child—I cannot ignore what he/she is saying or their actions." Fear becomes the control. "Will there be a fury of attack against me if I tell anyone of this? Will they whisper among themselves as we walk by?" These are the things that go through our minds when our children show signs of remembering past lives.

Fear becomes ever present in our reality. This fear cripples us, and if we do not step outside our mainstream box and find answers, it will keep us and our child from experiencing new things and learning that life is not temporary, that like many things from the past that evolve, grow, and change, new discoveries are made, old beliefs also change, and the way we look at life becomes different. Our children—who are enlightening us to this new perspective of life, death, and rebirth—have shown us that death is not something to fear. It is a way to live, evolve, come back, and journey on again and again. Our young children are our messengers from the past; as they tell these stories of remembrance, we learn. They are our teachers. They teach us how to live life from within and show us that we are souls that give life to each new body, each new beginning. They teach us that our lives have purpose, with an awareness of the loving beings that we are. They teach us that there is more than just life and death and that our soul consciousness holds within it many lives and lessons and that it is of pure love—if only we could open ourselves enough to see and hear it.

No matter what culture you came from or what religion you were brought up in, it is universally believed that since the beginning of conception, mothers have psychic connections with the souls of their children. So why would this change at birth? This belief was not created by such cultures as something that is either true or false. It is emphatically excepted *as is*. If we believe in this connection, then we should also believe in their truth and not fear "what they may say." The evidence of this lies in the stories of the children. Do not let fear get in the way. Do not miss the message in fear of what "they will say" because these memories do not last but for a few short years.

> *Past-life fears lurk beneath the surface of every individual.*
> *They are the reminder of the soul's past and how each life*
> *[affects] the other.*

— Ainslie McLeod, *The Instruction: Living the Life Your Soul Intended*

Real Fear from Past Life

Past lives, after our children's memories of them fade as they become mainstreamed into our earthly world and become human grounded through religion and culture, get hidden in our soul's consciousness, but the fear of the events and death of that past life can cause imbalance in this lifetime. Some consequences of this imbalance may be phobias, and an event in this lifetime may act as a reminder. Many of your soul's fears are related to its emotional state at the time of death in the previous lifetime. Sometimes these fears are nudges from your soul as a reminder that this is not something you want to repeat or vice versa.

Other irrational fears are a result of your soul's many incarnations. For a child, he or she may have separation anxiety when his or her mother leaves the house because the child is terrified that the mother will never come back or they will never see their mother again.

One of my clients told me a story in her regression about a past life where her daughter was her son in the time of Adolf Hitler in Germany at the time of the Third Reich, when they indoctrinated children into the Nazi Organization of the Youth. She did not approve of this and was looked at as an obstacle for Hitler's plans to instill his ideology among the youth. Her child was taken and put into a camp, and they were separated and never saw each other again. Most of these fears that we carry into another lifetime are the pain that was imprinted on our soul, such as the betrayal of someone we deeply loved, and it will show up in this lifetime as mistrust in people. That mistrust can show up as early as the first few months in life.

I have discovered in the years that I have spent doing past-life regressions in between lives, present lives and future lives, helping people uncover memories from their past lives that have carried over into their present lives emotionally or energetically, that these have caused the fears that they were born with in this lifetime. My goal in the regression is to help them remember past lives that are being held energetically and unconsciously in the soul–mind–body connection and that had been triggered in detail and then separate that experience from this lifetime.

Locked

When I was a young child, around the age of two years old, I had gotten locked in a closet. That memory was once triggered by a counseling session to help me rid myself of negative emotions that I was carrying around with me through my twenties. I thought I was okay with the memory and had no emotional attachment to it until one day, when I was in my room in an old house we were renting.

It was early in the summer season, but it was the first hot and sticky day. I had been writing in my room and listening to some music on my stereo, and so as not to disturb the rest of the house, I closed my door. My son had decided to go hang out with some of his friends, and everyone else was working. So eventually, I had the whole house to myself. A good hour or so went by, and it got hot. I was parched, so I got up to go downstairs to get some water, and I could not open the door. I went to turn the doorknob, and the screws were loose and fell out, along with the doorknob. I tried opening it by pulling the slide latch as leverage. I pulled, and the door would not budge.

The humidity and heat from the day made the door swell, and there I was, in a full-blown panic attack. I pounded on the door and screamed for help. I tried to open the window to yell out to someone to come help me, but the heat had made that sticky as well. I fell to the floor in a panic and cried like a scared child. My mouth was drier than sand, and I had thought that I would die in this room. I was in such a panic, I started having an asthma attack. Then after what seemed like an eternity, my son came home, came right upstairs to ask me if he could have money for pizza with his friends, and just pushed the door open, and I ran out.

After that day, I decided to do a regression and find out if there was more to this memory than just a childhood memory. My discovery was that I had died in a fire in a past life from asphyxia. I connected with that phobia and traumatic event in my past life, called imprinting. I saw it through and separated from it in this lifetime; now I do not have that fear. This is not to say that at another time, panic might start to arise, but now it is known, where and why, and you can separate yourself from those emotions and stop the panic.

I also learned that I did not have that fear in the closet when I was a toddler; I had not learned what fear was yet. To me, being locked in a closet was a regular event, a normal thing. I learned about this fear through imprinting and regression.

The Stunt Pilot

Sophia's son, Cooper, was going to be eighteen years old, and she wanted to get him something special to mark the occasion. The one thing she knew was that he had this love for and connection to airplanes, and he would always play games where he was a pilot on a big passenger plane. Growing up, he would put together model airplanes, and when he was sixteen, his mother had even gotten him a model remote-control airplane that took him a year to build, but he loved it so much, always looking at the skies, dreaming about the day he would fly his own real airplane. So for his eighteenth birthday, she had arranged for him to go to the airport and sign up for flight lessons, and he would be able to take one of the planes for a test flight with a skilled pilot. He was so excited.

So on the day of his birthday, Sophia took her son down to the airport for his surprise. The airport was filled with airplanes coming in and out that day, and they were getting set up for an air show that was coming to town in a week. Sophia went and signed her son up for nine months of flight school. The instructor welcomed him to the class and dressed him up and, when he was ready, took him for a tour of the tarmac. Then they went to board the plane they were about to fly.

This was like a dream come true for Sophia's son, and she felt like the best mom in the world. What a joyous moment! She felt the excitement and joy that Cooper was feeling at that moment.

They stepped on the tarmac, and over them flew a 747 passenger airplane coming in for a landing. Cooper, Sophia's son, immediately squat down to the ground and pulled his legs into a curled-up position on the runway, shaking like a frightened little boy, gasping for air and trying to breathe.

"Get me out of here! Help me!"

Sophia and the instructor picked up Cooper and brought him inside the building to calm him down. Cooper was so upset; after all, this had been something he dreamed about all his life. He could not even step into the plane, and he feared he would never be able to fly an airplane.

Sophia took him to the doctors to make sure there was not something physically wrong with him because he had described the feeling of his body hurting during that time of panic. Sophia thought that maybe that pain was just his panic attack and the tightening of his muscles. The doctor cleared him of any medical issue. So Sophia decided to do some research and discovered that past-life trauma could cause this type of panic.

Sophia called me, and we set up a regression. In Cooper's regression, he remembered being a pilot in the early 1900s. He was part of a team of pilots who did stunts. He was good, and he loved it. One day, during a training session, his plane started to stall, went into a tailspin, and crashed. He was taken to the hospital, where he died from his injuries. They said he had the love of the pilot in his blood and in his soul, and that did prove to be the case because Cooper carried that love over into this lifetime he was in.

I spoke with Cooper a few months later to find that he is doing well. He does not have emotional panic attacks anymore and was able to begin his flight school. He is more anxious than ever to complete his flight school so he can hit the airways. He also hopes to find a stunt team so he could once again do air stunts for spectators to watch and cheer him on.

The Soldier Within

Historical events could be another trigger, and just watching a documentary on television could cause a strong emotional reaction or the release of facts about the time. I even had a client named Roger who loved to watch old war movies, but during some of the battles, he would feel pain in his left leg and hip. His wife thought that he was so engrossed in the movie that he would get sympathy pains, so she would at times just give him an aspirin to ease the pain and brush it off as such. When it came time for him to go for his physical, his wife wanted to make sure that he did not have a medical reason for his pain. So she asked the doctor to perform some tests even though he too thought that they were just sympathy pains. Here is his story.

Roger was a younger man, so he was never drafted; nor did he ever volunteer to sign up for any military service. He went right from high school to college for an engineering degree. Roger was born with a birthmark that looked like a large scar on his hip, but he was never injured; he would jokingly call it his war wound. When the MRI came back, sure enough, there was nothing medically found. The doctor did question something that looked like an old scar from a previous injury, but Roger never had any such injury. This time, after the tests with the doctor, the pain remained. For months, Roger walked with a limp, and his wife had to give him aspirin more and more for the pain. Roger went to the library to see if he could find out the reason this was happening. He too started to believe that it was all in his head, that in some way, he was making this all up and creating these symptoms. He tried meditating, he tried yoga, and he even went to physical therapy. Nothing worked.

One day, during his research, he came across Dr. Brian Weiss and his study on the effects of reincarnation and how people can carry with them their wounds from a past life into their present life. He read cases where the patient went back into a past life through regression and healed themselves through the acknowledgment of the past life. This, to Roger, seemed like a magic trick and totally unrealistic, not to mention that he was brought up to be a man of faith and he was a true believer in his faith; this was just something he believed only atheists and nonbelievers in God would accept. Roger even felt guilty reading about such things. Past lives meant reincarnation, and that was unacceptable.

As Roger thought about the idea of past lives, his mind went back to when he was a child and the memories he had and how he had gotten so intrigued about wartime. Roger even sat down with his mother and asked her if she ever remembered how he had become so interested in the wars and how it had become such an addiction to him. She told him that he used to tell her stories about the wars.

He would say, "Mommy, when I was big, I fought in many wars, mainly WWI and WWII."

She told Roger, "And you always played army and never had enough army men, but as you got older, you stopped telling me your stories."

A few weeks later, Roger made the decision to explore reincarnation. He was reluctant, but he just needed to find the answers, even if it meant ruling out the possibility. We set up three sessions so we could prepare. Roger had never meditated before, and I needed to make sure he was comfortable and was not afraid of the journey. I wanted him to know that he controlled the journey and that he could awaken anytime, and going through the process a few times would reassure him of that. The day of the regression, I told Roger that I wanted him to come earlier than planned so that we could talk about the process.

"I felt that it was important to discuss your reasons for this regression, your concerns about your faith, and what we will be doing here today," I said. I explained that the gateway to a past life can be a spiritual experience since it is connected to the subconscious mind. "The interior process can be transforming for most. Through regression, the mind becomes a passage that, in time, you will use to find your way into deeper and more transcendent states. When you contact your deeper dimensions, you will experience a heightened awareness and a feeling of bliss. When I bring you back to the past life where you received the injury to your leg, it will be clear to you, where you are. Take the time to look around. This feeling is common to the soul. The feeling is familiar and is unique to you. You will go deeply into the spiritual realm, as deep as possible for you. You will be able to control everything you see. You are not constrained by time, and you can visit as many past lives as you would like. If your mind starts to wander and you lose focus, it is normal. All you need to do is gently return to your focus. The purpose of this journey is to discover your past life that gave you the leg and hip injury."

In Roger's brief review of his past life, he found himself in the fields of Western Europe during WWII, where he lost his life when he was wounded with a gunshot to his left hip that left him incapacitated and later succumbed to his injury. After Roger explored all that he wanted to in that past life, I slowly brought him back out. Through our post-regression discussion, I found Roger to be emotional and very reminiscent of his time as a soldier. During that time, he was deeply passionate, and although it was in another life, Roger felt a sense of pride, and it gave him the validation he knew inside. He knew his past life was a part of him and a part of history.

Over the next few weeks, the changes in Roger were very apparent to his family. The pain in his left hip and leg was gone, and he no longer walked with a limp now that he knew the root cause. He made peace with his religious beliefs, and as he told his stories of WWII, he spoke from his soul.

ONKYO

THIS REALITY IS not something new and not something that happens to a select few. This is part of the circle of life, death, and rebirth that is just unrecognized. The soul, before birth, scans the lifetime of more than one human being within the same time cycle before choosing the life lessons they need to learn and choose the best parents and life that can help them learn their lesson. Most children just have a spontaneous thought or conscious memory. Most fade back into the consciousness after the soul is grounded to the body. Some children will be more detailed with facts, and others may just have bursts of momentary thought.

One of my three-year-old clients had one of many momentary spontaneous memories when a package was delivered to his home that contained equipment for podcasting. When he opened the package, this little guy burst out with an excitement related to opening up a birthday or Christmas gift.

"Onkyo!" he exclaimed, which is a brand of stereo equipment that a deceased family member had and loved.

This young child had never heard of this brand or this type of equipment before, and just for reference, the equipment was not the Onkyo brand in the box, but that was what his memory had told him. When the equipment was taken out of the box, this three-year-old put it together. He knew where each piece needed to be plugged into, how to turn it on, and how to record with it. He had never been shown this before.

When he was done, he said with excitement, "I always wanted one of these. When I was big, I bought one!"

This is a good example of a past-life memory that was triggered by a piece of stereo equipment. There are many things that can cause a soul/personality past-life memory. This three-year-old was believed to be a family member who had passed suddenly three years before he was born. He was his mother's brother. One of his uncles' passions was audio equipment, and his hobby was videography and photography. He had traveled the United States, seeing all the major sites, like the rainforests and all the national forests and New Orleans at Mardi Gras, where he finished up his tour with exotic drinks, bead necklaces, and delicious food. Whenever he went somewhere to eat on his adventure, his motto was that he was not going to eat anything that he could have at home, and he enjoyed the finest. He spent six months on the road, finding himself and doing what he did best—taking videos and pictures.

When a magazine came in the mail, the little three-year-old would point out places that looked like where his deceased family member had traveled and taken pictures. One of the pictures he had pointed out was a picture of the Hoover Dam, and as his mother went through some pictures in some of her brother's stuff that was packed up after he had passed, she found a picture of him with his best friend at the Hoover Dam—the exact picture that was in the magazine. He would tell stories about when he was big, and he put beads around other people's necks and danced with masked, costumed people. These memories gave his mother comfort and opened her eyes to the concept of reincarnation and past lives. It helped her embrace her own past life and healing.

PEOPLE IN HISTORY WHO
BELIEVED IN PAST LIVES

Edgar Cayce: He was born on March 18, 1877, and died on January 3, 1945. A self-professed clairvoyant, he founded the Association of Research and Enlightenment Inc., also known as the ARE, in Virginia Beach, Virginia. He believed he was a resident of Atlantis in one of his previous lives.

Benjamin Franklin: One of the Founding Fathers of the United States, he was a Freemason at an early age and became the grandmaster of the State of Pennsylvania in 1734 and the secretary of his lodge, St. John's Lodge, in 1735–1738. He wrote in a letter to Ms. Hubbard on the occasion of his brother's death on February 23, 1756, "A man is not completely born until he is dead. Why then should we grieve that a new child is born among the immortals, a new member added to their happy society?" Benjamin Franklin believed in the transmigration of the soul at a young age of twenty-two, although it did not become known as reincarnation until after his death, in 1945. His belief in reincarnation was believed to have been exposed when he wrote about his return at the age of twenty-two, where he wrote his own epitaph, which history entitled "the most famous epitaph of America":

> *The Body of B. Franklin, Printer: Like the cover of an old book, its contents torn out and stripped of its lettering and gilding, lies here food for worms, but the work shall not be lost, for it will, as he believed, appear once more in a new and more elegant edition, revised and corrected by the author.*

Henry Ford: He was born on July 30, 1863, and died on April 7, 1947, the founder of the Ford Motor Company and the chief developer of the assembly line technique of mass production that revolutionized the automotive industry. In an interview with the *San Francisco Examiner* on August 26, 1928, Henry Ford exposed his belief in reincarnation in a statement: "I adopted the theory of reincarnation when I was twenty-six." He went on to state that "religion offered nothing to the point." He felt that he had uncovered a universal plan and that he then realized that there was a chance for him to work out his ideas. Believing that time is never-ending and no longer limited, he stated that the belief in reincarnation put his mind at ease, and he wanted this message to be shared with all men so that it too would put their minds at ease. Henry Ford was also convinced that he had been a soldier at the Battle of Gettysburg, where in that previous life, he had died.

Gen. George S. Patton: General Patton, commander of the U.S. Third Army, was an avid believer in reincarnation, along with some of his family. Although he had never entirely expressed this belief, he did believe that he would die in battle and return to lead the armies into battle in another life. He had many visions of many lives, and these visions began when he was a child and continued until his death at the age of sixty in 1945, this time not in battle. In his poem "Through a Glass, Darkly," he stated,

> So forever in the future
> Shall I battle as of yore,
> Dying to be born a fighter
> But to die again once more

A S A CHILD, he believed he had fought in the Turkish army and was killed by many arrows to the neck. In the Battle of Crécy in 1346, Patton believed he had fought along with John of Bohemia, a.k.a. John the Blind, as a French knight when they had lost the battle against the English. Both the knight and John of Bohemia died in the battle. Young Patton remembered dying by an impaled lance from the English. As Patton got older, he would remember more past lives, all of which were battles. He believed that this knowledge carried him through many lifetimes and helped him in his current life.

This is a central belief among New Age believers as well as spiritualists today. As more children are being acknowledged and not brushed off as having wild imaginations and the need to expand one's knowledge and accept the possibility of past lives grows, the journey of the soul is slowly discovered. Patton was viewed throughout his lifetime as maybe having mental issues because of his visions. Could he have been remembering his past lives?

Just like Henry Ford, Edgar Cayce, and General Patton, people who remember their past lives do it without any effort or trauma on their own part. Children especially just say, "Mommy, when I was big."

SIGNS THAT YOUR CHILD IS
HAVING A PAST-LIFE MEMORY

CHILDREN ARE MORE likely to remember past lives in detail than adults. Children are new to this lifetime, and their past lives are more recent than adults' past lives, and children are not yet mainstreamed. I have been asked by many parents, "How do I know that my child remembers a past life and that it is not his or her active imagination?" My first comment to this question is does your child act differently? Does he or she walk the walk? You can tell much by the actions of the child. Here are a few more things to recognize:

1. Is your child's understanding or knowledge beyond his or her years of age?
2. Does he or she have any birthmarks? Not all birthmarks are from a past life, but it is important to take notice for future identification. Thirty-five percent of children who claim to remember previous lives have birthmarks or birth defects that they attribute to wounds on people whose lives they remember.
3. Does your child have recurring nightmares? A nightmare is a common thing in life, and for children, sometimes it can be a hidden fear, so it is important to talk to your child and listen to their words. How are they speaking—in the past tense or in the present tense? Are the bad dreams happening on a regular basis? If yes and if the nightmare has nothing to do with their current life, a past-life memory could be triggering the nightmare. Do they have reoccurring nightmares over a significant amount of time that are often out of place in relation to other dreams? If the dream does not have any relevance in today's life, it can be a clue to a past life, especially if the dream relates to a different significant period other than the one in which they are living.

4. Does your child have unexplained phobias—the fear of butterflies and other insects, the fear of water, the fear of flying, the fear of being touched, the fear of certain people, and so on?

5. Does your child recognize or describe people or situations that do not pertain to his or her life? Does he or she identify photos of people who are deceased or whom they have never met?

6. Does your child have wisdom that is uncharacteristic or way beyond their own age or background?

7. Is your child's tone when describing his or her past life matter-of-fact and very consistent?

8. Does your child have the corresponding behavior and traits of the past-life memory (such as in play, where they can reenact the memories in their play)?

9. Does your child speak or understand another language (e.g., "My son speaks German in his sleep and does not know German," "One of my granddaughter's first words as she slammed her fist down on the high chair was *nein* (the German word for "no"), and she did it repeatedly")?

10. Does your child repeat the memory more than once, and is the basic information of the story the same?

11. Is your child's story not a repetition of someone else's story that he or she could have overheard?

12. Does your child speak of historical events that happened before they were born?

13. Does your child have talents that they were never, in this lifetime, trained to have?

14. Does your child say things like "Mommy, when I was big," "Remember when I was your mother?" or "I was big, I fell asleep, and I woke up a baby"?

15. Does your child see things before they happen and advise others about things they are too young to know about? Do they draw on experiences and lessons that they remember from previous lifetimes?

There is no right or wrong answer in knowing if your child is having a past-life memory, but the most basic of rules is if it is not of the normal present-life memory, then take notice and document.

Children who are in this lifetime are still infants and young, but their soul has journeyed through many lifetimes. Their bodies and minds are trying to navigate being here again on Earth, so although much of this is happening, their communication at such a young age can be hard to understand, and they may not make sense as they are trying to talk about their past-life memories. They may be giving you valuable information that you are simply not aware of. If your child starts talking about events in the past with much detail, take notice and listen. Do not assume that your child has an active imagination; they may just have an active memory. A child's mind is quiet and not yet filled with opinion, judgment, doubt, and conflict. They have not yet been mainstreamed in culture or religion. This purely quiet innocence is not yet ready to accept a reality that is imposed upon them by their parents and family circle. Part of them is still connected to their past life and the in-between. They remember choosing their parents, and they have the advantage. They speak the truth and recall their memories without being worried about being judged.

Listening to a child speak about their past-life memory, I can describe them as being enthusiastic. They love to tell their story, and I enjoy listening to them, so I sit and play with them as they get excited about telling me about their other life "when they were big." They speak so innocently and knowingly about living a life before this one. Some have even described what happened after their past death and on their journey to rebirth. I found it important to be in their world, totally engaged in their active memory.

When I have asked parents how they felt when their children started speaking of lives previous to the ones they were in, many parents would say that it "jolted them out of spiritual complacency and forced them to reconsider their own beliefs." As a past-life regression therapist, I always recommend for the parent to not let their present beliefs cloud the realization of their child's past-life journey. The understanding of their past life can offer insight into their future quirks and unexplained behavior. Many times, the parents have no explanation and just chalk it off as a mystery. Children, like everyone else, carry their memories in their consciousness and can hide within them and come out by acting them out in a physical way, such as fears and phobias, trust issues that can be very disruptive in the children's lives. These memories can also be a source of your child's strengths, skills, and talents in this lifetime. They are called inherited patterns of past lives, and these patterns get modified by experiences they had from each lifetime. When I say "inherited," I am not talking about family inheritance through bloodlines. I am talking about past-life inheritance, from one life to the next. Children remember these patterns because they are close enough to the surface of their conscious awareness, making accessing them easy. As the child gets older, their consciousness changes, and the memories get stored in the Akashic records to register and keep every change and choice made by the soul, becoming part of the universe.

PAST-LIFE PATTERNS

THERE ARE MANY children who do not speak of their past lives but show other signs that are indicators of past lives. It is believed that few people spontaneously recall past lives without some sort of trigger because of the memory loss that is typical in between the present lifetime and the past lifetime. When our soul is connected at birth to our body, it imprints the memories onto the new body, along with our emotions. Our emotions become the trigger for the soul, our radar, giving us specific urges and ideas to guide us as new humans in our chosen path for the present incarnation. Also, this can be recognized as our gut. Some of these triggers are as follows:

Unexplained Reactions to Strangers A child can see the past life from another person and can feel the energy, good or bad, in that person. It is a common belief that if a child screams or feels something that might be negative, that person is an evil person. This is not necessarily true. There are many explanations to this reaction, and one is that the energy around the person could be negative. Depression and anger could be the energy the child picks up.

Irrational Reaction to an Object

I have this attraction to antique shops and books. When I walk into an antique shop, I can feel the energy that is within the items in the shop. Many times, I get drawn to a specific item. I just have to hold it, feel its energy, and get pictures of the past. There have been times as well when the item feels like it's mine. You know that feeling when you lose something special or meaningful and suddenly find it? That is the feeling I get. If I do not buy it and take it home with me, I will dream and dream about it, and I feel that must go back and get it. When I bring it home, I get this feeling of completeness. I then meditate and travel back to where it was mine in a past life.

Irrational Reaction to a Place It was eight years after Louise's son had died tragically in a car accident, and it was the first time her grandson, Austin, would come to her house. She had always made the four-hour-long drive to visit her daughter and her family. This time, they were coming to visit her. Louise, since the loss of her son, had not had many people come to her house. It was her home, and it was filled with many memories that were precious to her. She did not want anyone to judge her. It had been a few months since she saw Austin, and Louise was excited. Carol, Louise's daughter, and Austin were the only ones coming because Jack, Carol's husband, was away on business, and Carol just needed a little getaway time. Louise lived in a four-bedroom home with plenty of space and rooms for Carol and Austin to sleep. As soon as they pulled in the driveway, Austin was out of the car and in the house.

He looked at Louis and said with such excitement, "I am home! I am home!" He ran right upstairs and into Mark's room, jumped up on the bed, and let out a sigh. "My room."

He sat there, just taking it all in like he was remembering it all. Austin was almost five years old and had not been born yet when Mark had his car accident.

"You saved all my stuff," he said as he looked around the room, which had not been touched except for normal cleaning.

Austin then climbed on the desk to the shelf. Taped to the bottom of a jar, hidden, was a key, the key to the desk. Louise never knew where the key was, and she had never bothered to open the drawer. Austin opened the drawer, went to the bottom, under all the stuff, and pulled out an old worn teddy bear.

Louise gasped. "That is Mark's teddy bear when he was a young boy. I thought he got rid of it." She hugged it as tears from many years of grief rolled down her face. She knew now that Mark had come back. "This is yours now, Austin. I hope he gives you many sweet dreams."

Instant Like/Dislike for Someone They Have Just Met

Billy was only two when he met Albert. Albert was the grandfather of his uncle and the father of his grandfather. Albert lost his wife two weeks before Billy was born and his youngest son four years before that. Albert came to visit and stayed for a week with his eldest son and his family once a year. Billy had seen pictures of him hanging in the living room of his grandparents' house, and he would point at the picture and say, "Mom and Dad."

When he met Albert, he looked at him and said, "Hi, Dad," and he would follow Albert around the house and outside, anywhere he went.

At lunchtime, Billy was sitting on his grandmother's lap, drinking his sippy cup, when suddenly, he got off her lap, went over to Albert, who was sitting in the chair on the porch, put both of his hands on Albert's face softly, looked into his eyes, and kissed him—a stranger whom he called Dad.

*   *   *

Sydney was two years old when her grandmother noticed that she had abilities that were starting to become more relevant as she grew. As a baby, when they used to take her places, Sydney would cry nonstop in places where she felt uncomfortable. As soon as they would leave these places, Sydney would stop crying. Sydney did not like loud voices or loud noises and, at the sound, would bury her head and cry. As she got older, she would cover her ears.

When her mother went on a business trip and Sydney had to stay with her grandmother, Sydney was so happy and was such a good little girl. One day a friend of her grandmother's came over to visit, and the moment he came to the door, Sydney ran to her grandmother, buried her head, and cried.

"What a beautiful little girl she is," the friend said, trying to warm Sydney up to him, but the closer he got to her grandmother, the louder and more aggressively she would scream.

When he left, she was fine, the crying stopped, and she went back to play.

A Connection to a Picture from the Past When Zachary was one year old, his father unpacked some old family pictures that his mother had and that his dad had given him when his mother journeyed on. "See, Zachary? This is your family who left us before you were born."

Zachary pointed to a picture of his father's mother and said, "Mommy," to his father's mother, who had passed a week before Zachary was born.

"Do you see Uncle Mike in these pictures?"

Zachary pointed to his father's uncle Mike.

"Do you see Aunt Betty?"

Zachary looked at the picture and pointed to a woman in a picture of five other women—right at Aunt Betty. Zachary went on to identify all six relatives who had passed and whom he had never met or seen pictures of before.

Allergies

Unexplained allergies are known to be connected to a past life, specifically relating to being poisoned in a past life. The allergy could be food, a beverage, even smells. It could even be a resistance to taking medicine of any kind or vitamins, minerals, or any other supplement. It is the body's way of alerting and avoiding past-life poisons.

Asthma

Unexplained asthma attacks could be the result of having been suffocated or gassed to death in a past life. It is also a sign of being burned in a fire.

A woman was referred to me because of her son having traumatic nightmares where he would gasp for air and fight in bed like he was fighting his way out of something, and when he would awaken, he would have a full-blown asthma attack. When this first started for the son, around the age of two, the mother took her son to the doctor. The doctor decided not to treat this right away and said that when it happened again, the mother was to put him in a bathroom with steam to try a natural way of relieving his asthma. So when it happened again, by the advice of the doctor, she filled the bathroom up with steam and brought her son in to ease the asthma.

Her son screamed, "Help! I am in here! Get me out!" His arms were slashing the air, trying to part the mist as he was in a panic of feeling trapped.

His asthma continued. His mother helped and soothed him. The next day, changing him and trying to hold him down turned into a traumatic experience. Doctors could not figure out what was going on. There was no medical reason why this was happening. This all launched a state investigation in fear of abuse. They also found no reason and surely no abuse.

Things started to come together when he was with his secondary caretaker while his parents worked. The caretaker, unknown to her, had something that had spilled over in the oven prior to her baking cookies, and when she turned on the oven, it started to smoke up the kitchen and the downstairs area. The little boy saw this, smelled the smoke, screamed in a panic, and ran right out of the door.

"Help! Get me out!" He dropped to the ground and went right into an asthma attack.

The caretaker ran out and grabbed him to soothe him, and he screamed more—"Get this off me! I am stuck!"

His mother was called out of work. When she got there, he got up and into her arms and wrapped his arms around her neck. She sat there, just rocking him. Soon, the asthma stopped, and he was back to normal. Then they were referred to me.

Let me take this out of the equation, I do not do past-life regressions on children for many reasons, one being that I have not come up with a technique that can actually settle a child down enough to do a regression. Another, more important reason is that the trauma they could open could be devastating. When dealing with children, I choose to use facts and behavior and then connect all the dots. When that is done, we need to connect the story to the child to help him or her relate and make a soul connection to complete the trauma. This is not a scientifically proven remedy. It is not in some medical book. It is a technique I have used that has worked with all my young cases and some older cases. It starts with the interview of the parents and documenting all the evidence, with the child finding different scenarios of play to observe and interact with. This sets the child in a calm atmosphere where they can act out stories and where the child is at ease to talk to you about it.

From the interview, the evidence showed that this young boy might have, in a previous lifetime, died in a fire where he was trapped. That was my determination. My next step was to determine the best staged play area that would not put this little guy into panic mode. With this information, I set up a play area with videos, books, and toys that would represent what I felt was a sympathetic, interactive play area. He engaged with it very well. Mom and I sat there, playing with him, listening to him as he interacted with the toys, telling us stories that might seem to come from a child's imagination.

He used names and technical terms for the equipment, knowing each gadget of the fire truck, saying things like "When I was big, I did this, and this guy was my buddy."

"Did you drive a fire truck?" we asked.

"Yes," he said. "Number 24."

We showed him pictures of fire trucks and fire hats and boots. Soon, we were able to identify the period. Mom found out that there was a day for the kids at the local fire department, so she brought him there to see the trucks. They had some of the older-style trucks there on show as well. He was so excited. One of the firemen came over, and his mom asked if he could sit inside the fire truck, and the fireman lifted him up and allowed him to be in the truck.

The little boy sat back in the seat and gave a sigh. "Ahhh, my old friend." Then he sat up and grabbed the steering wheel like he was going to drive the fire truck. "Let's go, Bob!" he said as he made siren sounds.

He looked over at the instruments in the truck and explained what each one was for correctly. He was so excited, like any little boy would be, but he was four years old and had never had any knowledge of old fire trucks, living in a country where tractors were a little boy's dream.

After this, we gathered all the information for his story and analyzed it. I put together all the data from the session, and we got together one more time. I had put together a storybook to read to this little fireman, one that he could have a soul connection with using the names and events he had mentioned in his session, and I told him his story. I had made this DYI storybook of his story as a keepsake and asked him if I could read it to him, *The Story of a Hero Fireman*.

"Is that the story of when I was big? I was a hero?"

"Yes, little guy, it is," I said, "and it is yours to keep."

This process helped my client and her son relieve the trauma of a past life. In many past lives, especially those with children, it is not always necessary to identify the exact person in their past lives. That can take years. Many people die from the same type of death, but the goal is to heal the trauma brought over into this lifetime from a past life they remember. The documenting of their story gives them the information they can continue later if they choose to take it further.

I am happy to say that this little guy has never had an asthma attack, nightmare, or panic attack again to this date. The boy, at the time of this writing, is now ten years old.

Chronic Pain and Fatigue

If not linked to a present medical reason, chronic pain or fatigue is often the result of a past-life trauma. The location of the pain is where the wound was in a past life. It is my belief that when a soul connects to the new vessel, the body, it plugs into all of the soul's memories and downloads all the memories, and the body remembers, such as in cellular memory. Unhealed trauma can trigger the pain of the past-life injury. This can happen with souls that did not take enough time in the shower of healing before reincarnating into other lives and that had not had enough time before reincarnating into the next lifetime. A memory trigger from a past-life or present-life trauma could trigger the pain from the injury where there is no apparent reason for the chronic pain. [This is also explained in *Through the Cracks: The Magic in Me* (2017) and *Faded: Circle of Life to the Soul* (2019).]

Fears (Terror)

Does your child have a fear of the dark. Does he or she avoid getting out of bed when it is dark for no apparent reason? Does he or she fear water or have any irrational fear that has no reason in this lifetime?

Fear of Accidents

In the case of Owl Phoenix, at the age of two, he started to develop a fear of riding a car. When he would see a car turn out in front of his mother's car to pull into traffic, he would, from the back seat, scream, "Watch out!"

Through research, I discovered that in Owl Phoenix's recent past life, he was killed when an intoxicated driver made a wrong turn across traffic and hit him, and he never gained consciousness and succumbed to his injuries a month and a half later. When we told Owl Phoenix this story in a relatable "once upon a time" story and he received a motorized motorcycle as a Christmas present, he related to it, and the terrifying screams stopped.

Avoiding Physical Touch

A woman called me and asked me if she could come and talk to me about her husband. Through their years of courting and their few years of marriage, she stated that her husband did not like being touched. His mother had asked the doctor about this when he was young, and there was never any identifiable medical explanation as to why he did not like being touched without his permission. This was not a problem with intimacy in their marriage because that was something he expected. To touch him off guard or among crowds would result in him getting very upset. Sometimes, if he had to be in an area such as an elevator and could not avoid being touched, he would close his eyes and hold his breath. He was not the angry type; nor did he ever act in a violent matter. He just winced at the feel of being touched.

She had thought that maybe he was germophobic, but he was not. He believed that we need germs to survive. He also had dreams of terror that he described as spiraling dreams. He would, in his dream, be spiraling downward with a humming sound in a panic and suddenly be woken up with a flash of light in his dream. It was thought that maybe he was remembering his birth, but why was it a terrorizing dream, where he felt panic? That did not seem to make any sense. Her husband also had this desire to have a fan on all year long, and if they went to a hotel, he had to turn the air conditioner down to the lowest setting, and it froze her or anyone in the room.

She decided to look at more metaphysical and spiritual reasons as to why this was happening. I told her that she should ask him if he would be open to a past-life regression. A few days later, she called me, and we set up a past-life regression session and counselling. In my past-life regression therapy sessions, I inform the client that the process takes about two hours. I gave her a questionnaire to fill out, asking questions that went back to when he was a child. It was amazing how much information of his past life he had spoken about or acted out as a child that, until this session, never got put together or was acknowledged as information, not just the ranting and acting out of a young child. I send home meditation exercises to get the client ready for the regression. I find this greatly beneficial because of the fact that most people do not know how to meditate or do not feel comfortable with it. Getting acquainted with meditation helps one have a successful regression.

The day of the regression, we went over what would happen and what we were looking for, and after the regression, we talked about what he saw. Once the client was relaxed, very little suggestion was needed for the memory to come up.

The regression began with some light sounds of meditation bowls and soft music as I counted down to delta.

"As I count down, relax each part of your body," I said. "Ten . . . Breathe in to the count of four . . . Breathe out to the count of four . . .

nine . . . eight . . . seven . . . six . . . five . . . four . . . three . . . two . . . one. Now I am going to take you deeper . . . deeper . . . back to the womb . . . back to the life most traumatic . . ."

I asked him questions like where he was, what he saw, and what he was doing. I let him visit his past life for a while. Then I told him to fast-forward to his death. I instructed him on how he could step back and just view his death like a movie. This minimized the emotions of the death. After visiting a few lifetimes and deaths, we located where the trauma came from. I counted him back up. I gave him some water, and a piece of chocolate as we sat in silence for a few minutes to allow him to come back fully and process his experience.

When he was ready, we discussed his experience. He went on to describe being a pilot in a war. He remembered that day—boarding his plane, sitting in the cockpit, saying his prayer like many other men at war. He pulled out a picture of his wife and daughter. He told them he loved them as he kissed his picture and placed it back into his left pocket, closest to his heart. When I asked my client if he remembered what his wife and daughter looked like, he said yes. I asked him if he had met them again in this lifetime. With tears in his eyes, he said he had. His wife and daughter were now, in this lifetime, his cousin. He knew when they had met years back that they had known each other before, and the love was still there but could never be. When he saw the picture, he knew right away who they were in this life.

He had promised that he would return, and as the plane spun to a fiery crash, he said, "I love you!"

His death in that lifetime was the key to the reason he did not like being touched. Being touched in the present life, where the sufferer was injured or burned, can be very painful, like an itching under the skin that will not go away if someone touches them in the area of the past-life injury. We also discovered that his nighttime sweats and terror, resulting in always having to have a fan or air conditioner on at night, were also from the fiery crash. I explained to my client the benefits of having and knowing these past lives. Remembering past lives can correct the wrongs that have been done in these past lives so we do not have to relive them again in the present life. This regression also showed that we reincarnate with certain soul groups. His soul was able to recognize and reconnect with his wife and daughter in a previous life to heal. It also answered the question of how and why they were all connected the moment they had met. I sat there and let him tell me all that he saw and watched as his energy transformed and how excited he was to tell me these things.

I set him up for a follow-up session in a few weeks. When he came back to see me, he and his wife told me how much he had transformed. He did not have a touching issue anymore. Now he hugged everyone. He did not have any more nightmares of spiraling, and his fan only came on when it was summer. The terrifying nightmares went away, along with the humming sound. Her husband connected with his past life and, by doing so, was healed from the physical and emotional trauma stemming from that previous life. It also opened him up spiritually and vibrationally. The trauma that was passed over into this lifetime had created a block for him in his soul consciousness, which made it hard for him to evolve and increase his vibration, which unlocked the doors to his intuition and his soul consciousness. He was able to forgive himself for dying in the crash and leaving his wife and daughter alone. He flushed out what was no longer needed and plugged into the universal consciousness, where his awakening began. We now meet to work on his new life, the one he was born into.

Phobias about Death

More than 35 percent of souls reborn too soon after unnatural deaths in past lives develop phobias of death. Some of these unnatural deaths may include drowning and car accidents, where the death was instant. The phobia can appear when the child is incredibly young, like in the case of Jason.

Jason was still an infant when his mother had noticed that when Jason was restrained, even when simply having his diaper changed, he would panic and scream horribly. As he got older, he would continue to get worse. When Jason was about four years old, his brother had decided to join the wrestling team. His brother would come home and want to wrestle with his little brother Jason, showing him what he had learned at practice. At first, Jason was excited that his big brother wanted to play with him and show him some of his cool moves. There was a three-year age difference, so although his big brother would play with him when no one was around, when his friends would come around, his big brother would often go off with his friends, and Jason was just too little to play with them.

It was raining on this day, and their mother had just bought his brother a new wrestling mat to practice on. Jason wanted to wrestle; it looked like so much fun.

Jason's brother showed his little brother some of the stances and holds that his coach had taught him that day, and then they wrestled. Jason laughed and laughed and glided around the mat, letting his brother chase him. When his brother caught him, he pinned him on the mat, like wrestlers do, and instantly, Jason squirmed and squirmed.

He screamed, "Help! Anybody, help me! I am stuck! Get off!" He pushed his brother off him.

Their mother ran into the room where the boys were wrestling. "What is going on, boys?"

She looked in the corner of the room, and there was Jason, red-faced, tears running down his face, crying so hard, he was gasping for air. His mother went over to check if he was hurt in some way that may need medical attention. There were no visible injuries. She tried to hug him, and he pulled away, so like a mother would do, she sat there next to him, singing softly to him, waiting for him to calm down and want a hug from his mommy. Within time, he did calm down and want a gentle hug of love from his mother.

She asked him what had happened, and he said, "Mommy, when I was big, I couldn't move, and I died. You know, Mommy, when I was big like you. Remember, Mommy?"

Then he was off and running around with his brother, roughhousing like little boys do. Jason's mother sat there, wondering about what he had said and remembering how, since he was born, he would scream and panic whenever he was restrained. She had thought that maybe it was just a normal stage and that Jason was just an overactive child. Those words—"Mommy, when I was big" and "Remember, Mommy?"—just struck a chord in her. Jason was not playing make-believe; he was profoundly serious and thought she would remember. This rose concern in her, and she could not stop thinking about it. She decided to ask Jason about it.

One day, when her other son was at wrestling and she was alone with Jason, who was playing with Legos, she asked him, "Jason, do you remember when you were big like me and I was your mommy?"

"No, Mommy," he said. "You were not my mommy then. You were my brother. Remember? A tree came down on me, and I could not move. You cried and tried to get Mommy, and it took too long, and I died." He looked her in the eye and lovingly squeezed her face.

She was shocked to hear all that. That was not what she had expected, and it brought tears and chills through her body. His sincerity rocked her. *How could he remember all that, and how could I remember nothing?* she thought. She continued to play with Jason but did not ask any more questions. She was now so bewildered. She needed time to process this before she went any further.

That night, she called her friend over for a nice relaxing glass of wine. After all, she needed to trust someone with this, or she felt like she would go crazy. Maybe hearing herself talk to someone, just telling the story, would give her some clarity. After the boys were both in bed, she and her friend sat down and talked about what had happened, going back to even when Jason was an infant.

"Kids have overactive imaginations. Do you think that would be the case here?"

"No because I felt it deep. It was like when he looked into my eyes, I knew somehow he was telling me a truth he remembers."

Her friend suggested that she talk to her psychic friend who dealt with past lives.

"Past lives? Is that even real? I was brought up to believe that past lives are not real, that we only have one life." According to her beliefs, growing up, it is a sin to even read about reincarnation or past lives.

She made an appointment with me, and I told her of my beliefs and that there are many books and information out there that support this same belief. I added that my direction in past lives is not to identify who her son was in a past life by name but to educate her in helping him with his phobia so that he can release it and move forward from it. I thought that one of the best ways to do that in this situation was to connect her to that past life in which he had identified her as his past-life brother. I do not believe in putting children into a regression. I feel it could unlock some other traumas that are best suited for someone with a degree in child psychology. I did feel that if she were willing, I would regress her to that time, and in doing so, I knew from my experience that it would help her get knowledge of the past life to help her son clear his phobia. I also explained to her that Jason was four now and that in a few years, his memory of this life would fade, but the phobia could last. This was her decision. I sent her home with a few book recommendations and planned on meeting her again when she was ready for a follow-up. In the meantime, I suggested she write down any information that Jason would give her, with dates and times, just to help us if we chose to proceed.

This situation is hard to proceed with many times in my field because it is free will. Do you let the memory fade and deal with the trauma later, or do we find a way to let it go now? It is ultimately what is best for the family and child. It is important to consider that although the memories of the past lives fade and are stored in our Akashic records (I will explain that in the further chapters of this book), the emotion still remains and can cause emotional baggage not only in this lifetime but also in other lifetimes to come. This idea can be overwhelming for people with rooted belief systems. To be successful, they would need to be open to seeing this through. She told me that she grew up believing that we only lived one lifetime but was open for other ideas because she felt that her son was tormented and that for some reason, I was making sense to her.

A few weeks later, I got a phone call from her again, and she was ready to meet with me again. It is important to understand that for some people, regression is easy; for others, it takes time to get there.

She was one of the latter people. We worked on meditation and being able to reach where we needed to go, and finally, we did get her there in that life. When I brought her back, she felt overwhelmed, anxious, and elated at the same time. I gave her some water to let her flush through and process her emotions and some dark chocolate (dark chocolate helps in the grounding of energy). She now had her story. I suggested that she should make a friendly child enactment with some toys to release the trauma, like a fairy tale. When she did this, Jason had no more traumatic episodes, and the bond between mother and son grew even deeper. She continues to explore deeper into her consciousness and the spiritual component that links our lives.

Traumatic Events

Past-life memories can be triggered and jolted back into the present memory if the event was traumatic and is like what had been experienced in the past life. The memory usually does not make sense in this lifetime but might just carry some points that are similar. You could be going about your life in a natural manner. Then a smell or a sound, even something visual, happens, and all of a sudden, your mind is flooded with memories that do not seem to belong in this current life. Fears are not the only past-life triggers, but from what I have evaluated, they are the most common. Scents can be powerful because they trigger emotions. These patterns can cause present-life issues, such as subconscious body imprints, which means that the chronic pain that one has, such as in their shoulder, that has no pain memory in the present lifetime could come from a stabbing or gunshot wound in a past life and arise spontaneously in the present life. Some of the issues that are transferred from a past-life imprint can cause not only memory but imprinted emotional responses. Ainslie MacLeod—in his book *The Old Soul's Guidebook: Who You Are, Why You Are Here, and How to Navigate Life on Earth*—lists some of the causes and effects of imprint transfers:

- Fear of loss: a result of losing a loved one, something dear, or your money in a past life.

- Fear of betrayal/ mistrust: caused by infidelity or disloyalty in a past life.
- Fear of powerlessness/resisting being told what to do: caused by slavery or imprisonment in a past life.
- Fear of failure/lack of belief in your potential: caused by an incomplete or disappointing past life.

By recognizing these patterns, triggers, causes, and effects in our children when they are young, we can help them correct and leave behind imprints from the past life before they manifest into a combination of symptoms, including chronic dissociation, anxiety, fear, phobias, and many other post-traumatic stress disorders brought on by past-life memories.

TODAY'S AWAKENING

TODAY'S AWAKENING IS being experienced by the parents. The children are awakening the parents to what I feel is not so new of an energy pattern but more prevalent and stronger. Where few parents notice the words and actions of their children as anything but play or imagination in previous children, some parents even fear that their children are mentally challenged in some ways and find ways to medicate them.

In today's world, if you cannot figure it out and if it is what is labeled as "not of the norm," then for "safety," we need to medicate them. That is the common census. As parents, we trust and believe our doctors. They have that schooling, that degree that gives them that title, and that license to tell us what they feel these so-called abnormalities are. We live in the age of the "pill for everything." I am not downplaying the degree of a doctor. They are highly needed and very much professionals in their field, but not all children need medication. My personal and biggest pet peeve is ADHD medication. This is because the children today are all overly sensitive. We did not listen to them before, so now they are louder. They want to be heard. Medicating them blocks the energy pattern flow. Parents are noticing this oversensitivity and inability to focus in our children, and children are speaking and emphasizing more of what they see and feel.

Children are born multidimensional, and it takes years for them to adjust fully into this three-dimensional world. They are overly sensitive to begin with and react and cry at loud noises, at certain people, at certain times. They can feel emotions without words or actions. Until they are older and able and are mainstreamed into culture and religion, children have the freedom to let their consciousness travel wherever they choose and at any time they choose while still living in the present, in this three-dimensional world.

Sometimes, like I described before, children do not like being touched because that sensation makes them feel unsafe, and it is the person's energy that the child is reacting to. They feel everything that the other person has experienced. They can feel the person's deepest fears and feelings. They can feel their light and their darkness. As parents, sometimes we just do not understand this. It confuses us and makes us fearful. A young child may stray from someone who is depressed or has been drinking or feels anger. The child is imprinted by the mother and father, so the child is used to their emotions, but if a parent were to raise their voice when naturally, this is not a normal emotion, or action, the child will react. Why is it that we can accept this in an infant, who has not been taught emotion or has no understanding of it, but when the child gets a little older, around two years old, we question it and start to look for abnormalities or we look to religion to cast out the devil in them or any demon that might be making our child this way? We do everything we can to change this ability that they were born with instead of stepping outside the box and digging deep into our consciousness for the answers.

One of our biggest roadblocks is that as adults, we are taught to think in a linear manner, with logic. Everything must have a reason and a purpose. "He or she is doing this because . . ." "Why would he or she do this?" "There must be some human logic behind this." Children think compartmentally. They draw from their consciousness, which is stored in their soul consciousness and the Akashic records. They, like all of us, are born spiritual beings. Our bodies and our three-dimensional reality humanize us, and culture and religion mainstream us.

Children can come in and out of their soul consciousness. They are fully aware of alternate and multidimensional worlds. They have no chronological limitations and can switch and recall different lifetimes, including the world before their incarnation. They have been telling us this—when they see Grandma or Grandpa, who passed before they were born, or point them out in pictures they have never seen. They tell us this when they say, "Mommy, when I was big" or "Mommy, remember when we were big and we did this?"—those statements and many others.

One client told me her son was watching her put on makeup one day, and he said to her, "Mommy, I remember when you were Sue and I was Lizzy and we used to put on each other's makeup. That was fun! Remember, Mommy, when I was big like you? Sing that song we liked, Mommy. Remember?" and he would start to sing a song from years gone by.

These things do not happen as if they are living that past person's life. It is a glimpse into a memory that the soul remembers. Our children, at a young age, are telling us of their journey and their travels. More and more, each generation is born, and more and more, parents are awakening and hearing their children. It is now important that parents be educated enough to help in the evolving of the soul.

THEN WHO ARE WE?

Tune into that voice inside you, for it is truth.

OFTEN I HEAR people say that their child is a reincarnation of so and so. We will go more in depth about reincarnation later in this book, but the important thing is that in each lifetime, our soul carries the personality of the soul that was in the previous lifetime, meaning our personalities are relevantly the same throughout all our lifetimes, but your child is not Peter, who died years ago. He is Lucas, your son. He was Peter in another life, and it is stored in his consciousness. We are all universal travelers, going from lifetime to lifetime. Nothing is lost; it only changes. Each new journey gives us new challenges and new adventures, and each adventure has new things that shape us. In this lifetime, this humanness is just a speck on a continuous journey, and we collect different knowledge and different experiences on each journey. Our essence remains the same, so Peter's previous soul chose the birth and life of who is now Lucas. He will add to that journey. Some interests from the past will stay with Lucas (for example, prodigy children), and some will just be stored in the consciousness/Akashic records and could come out in another lifetime. The soul has imprints of previous lives that are carried on to each life. There has been much speculation as to gender, with a question as to whether we reincarnate into different genders or animals.

Ian Stevenson was a renowned scientist and author who had done extensive research on past lives. His data shows that approximately 10 percent of 1,200 cases of his validated reincarnation series of souls changed genders. In my opinion, this is valid proof that gender does and can change from lifetime to lifetime. As I did my research on this question on gender change, I added in my clients, and I discovered that all my clients who had more than one past-life memory also had lives in the opposite genders than their present genders. We need to remember and add to the mix the fact that a soul has no gender, so it would not establish a gender preference, and if we follow these masters in science who specialize in reincarnation and then add to the data collected by the ones who picked up where Stevenson had left off, such as Dr. Jim B. Tucker, and look at doctors in psychology, such as Dr. Brian Weis, we can see the pattern of evidence through clinical proof.

Our souls have free will, and not only do they choose their lessons, but also, they choose how these lessons would be achieved. Having free will also gives the soul the freedom to choose where it will reincarnate. This is not the only place where souls are. There are many different dimensions and different levels of consciousness. Earth is not the only school. Understanding this information will open doors for you to understand your child when he or she tells you they are happy that they chose you and when they describe unfamiliar places.

You have many skeptics, and within the mix are even scientists. The intriguing part of all this lies in the following question: how does basic science determine what information is carried in the soul? Science looks for physical proof. There are many other means and sciences that have linked the soul and the consciousness. The proof has been in the many near-death stories and the stories of thousands of children who remember their lives before they were born into this one. They remember these in great detail, and those children who have come to this lifetime with trauma, when acknowledged and worked with, have overcome these traumas. The hardest thing to accept is the understanding that this is their nature and their journey and that they chose this path and the gender they want to continue to this next journey.

To understand why so many awakened children are incarnating now, into this lifetime, you need to appreciate the role they are playing in the expansion of human consciousness. In doing so, you also have to understand that it is critical to first comprehend the bigger cycle at work that is driving our collective experience. These children are here to awaken and evolve humanity to its next level of consciousness. If you open your eyes to see and tune in with your ears to listen, you will begin to experience and embody the soulful wisdom that they bring to enlighten us in our everyday life and see the embodiment of our human blueprint, which is our fundamental truth and the vibration of that truth of who we are, showing us our natural state of consciousness. We have inherent within us the capacity for vision and transcendental experience, and our children awaken us to it to show us that we live each life and journey to the next and constantly evolve and grow. They awaken us to the soul, make us aware of our breath, and connects us deeply with the vital force energy that flows through us, births us, and is us.

*The Akashic records are a vast system of
organized energy that imparts the wisdom of
the ages.
It is rich, ever-changing awareness which delights
in the unique and inclusive universal expression of
consciousness.*

— Lumari, *Akashic Records: Collective Keepers of Divine Expression*

AKASHIC RECORDS

TO SOME, IT is strange to think that we live many lives with one soul and many bodies. Now imagine a record of all this stored in this universal consciousness, encoded in a nonphysical plane of existence called the etheric plane. They call this the Akashic records. Another name is the book of records, the Akashic field, or the zero-point field. This is where the records of our souls are stored in energetic form, a universal hard drive.

These records are like an immense photographic film, registering all the desires and earthly experiences of all souls. It holds the life of every human being and every living thing since time began. It is our energetic journal. Within these records are also stored our collective wisdom and the knowledge and skills we learned and accomplished in all our lives. That explains prodigy children and the knowing our children have and express to us at young ages. When we access these records, we can discover the exciting, absolute knowledge and experiences of our souls, as if they were part of a hard drive of cosmic information. We can discover not only our past but our present and future possibilities, leaving the doors open to help us connect the dots to our existence and putting reincarnation within our journey.

Edgar Cayce believed that the Akashic records were an invisible force field around the Earth, a boundless space. He believed this space was all-encompassing, encompassing everything in this etheric field. This etheric field he called the Akashic records has stored every action, emotion, thought, image, desire, journey, incarnation, and death and everything in between. He believed this record was available to all; you just had to reach it and open it. Cayce, in the twentieth century, was the most documented psychic and was believed to be a mystic who could connect with the etheric field. This was his essential talent, to connect with the invisible etheric force field, enter the hall of records, and access and describe information from the Akashic records.

Cayce not only believed it was possible to attune to the Akashic records but also believed this could occur frequently. If you were of this belief and were attuned to the universe, you could hear, read, and experience the information from these records. To many, this just seemed to be too astounding to be possible, and they never accessed these records. Cayce had a simpler way of explaining this without going into all the scientific and spiritual explanations:

When there is a thought or the activity of the body in any particular environ, this very activity makes for this impression upon the soul. As to the records made by such an activity, these are written upon what is known as time and space. In 1934, with one of his clients, Cayce tried to expand his explanation of the records by explaining how the Akashic records were written and how all humans could access their own information through the Akashic records. He went on to explain how each activity and thought in our lives produces a vibration, and that vibration makes a mark upon the skein of space and time, and it permanently identifies with the soul.

I have learned that this is a vibrational energy that we have within our soul, which, within itself, is energy. This vibration does not just leave a mark in space and time; it is also within our soul, and as we bond in this humanness, it becomes an imprint on one another's souls. That is why sometimes, with a stranger, we may feel that we knew them before but have never met them, good or bad. We imprint their soul in each lifetime. In earthly life, our actions can be constructive or destructive depending on the choices made by the person. This is all imprinted on the soul. Accessing the Akashic records allows us to take full advantage of the human experience and give us an understanding of how connected we are to others on this planet, on other planets, and in other dimensions.

The access point of these records starts with the mind. The mind, at any age, has access to these dimensions and can access these records. Many intuitive individuals have stated that children cannot access the Akashic records. They feel that children have nothing to gain and have no maturity or life experience, and the wisdom gained in the Akashic records would not be understood, but they forget that the soul has free will and that we are souls within bodies. Children are not little apprentice people on their way to adulthood. All children are spiritual beings born of an infinite system, with all the wisdom, power, and abilities from the universe in which they were born.

> Every person is whole and complete in the now, regardless of the chronological age of the body. (Dr. Wayne Dyer, *Memories from Heaven*)

I have been at the births of most of my grandchildren, and each time I saw them come into this world, I could see the spiritual beings that they are. In their eyes, I could see their essence and the wisdom they hold. When they open their eyes, even for just a second, to look at me, it is like we have known each other before. The confidence in their eyes shows no doubt of who they are, and they know that they have such value and purpose. I say to them, "Welcome, infinite one. I am happy to meet you and eager for the lessons you bring me." These little ones are a grand source of inspiration, and their souls already hold the wisdom of the Akashic records.

The souls of all humans are part of a universal consciousness. The mind might not be mature enough, but the soul is higher intelligence and has access to all past, present, and future events, and surely, a child can access the Akashic records even more easily than an adult. Young children can access them naturally until a certain age. It is familiar to them while they have the memory. They have past lives, future lives, and in-between lives to access, and their souls are not of infancy. In those records, they can access all those dimensions. Children do not have to learn how to release their minds and let go of mental programming and still maintain the enhanced connections of the universal consciousness. The soul is already at a high vibration coming into this lifetime. Some people have stated that this is the reason for autism or why some have died at a young age. We all were children once. We all entered this world the same way, with a high vibration, in my belief and according to my research. This is not accurate. Children do not get autism or die because of this high vibration. Children with autism already have higher vibrations than most, and they have incredible insight of the world around us and beyond if we just take the time to listen and talk to them and not dismiss them.

In my second book, *Faded: The Circle of Life to the Soul*, I spoke of a wonderful boy who was autistic and who had changed my life. Dr. Wayne Dyer says, "If you change the way you look at things, the things you look at change." Each person who comes into your life has a purpose and a lesson to teach you. Our children who have disabilities or early illnesses have lessons for us, and it starts with unconditional love and tolerance. They are our true angels, and they chose this for this lifetime. It is so hard to get their messages and lessons across in this "all about me" world we live in today. An autistic child needs to be taught on their terms with compassion, recognizing who they are. Dr. Meg Blackburn Losey describes this in her book *The Children of Now: Crystalline Children, Indigo Children, Star Kids, Angels on Earth, and the Phenomenon of Traditional Children*. For anyone with an autistic child, it is a must-read book. For anyone who is not judgmental or just wants a understanding of the idea, I highly recommend the book. As she states, these children are not disabled, just differently abled. They are utterly amazing. They see and remember far more than the mainstream person can. They can feel your energy and will react to chaotic energy or loud energy or voices that carry such energy. Many of them know and remember their past lives and in-between lives. If you allow them to be open and listen, they will tell you all about it. Their vibrations are so high, they can hear the light hum in the store, and to them, it is extreme. When you see them wearing noise-canceling headphones, it is because it hurts them to hear it. They are not violent and do not deserve to be restricted or cuffed. That torments them, and they do not understand. Get their focus, put a weighted blanket around them, and let them wear their headphones. It is like a hug and comforts them. The headphones help them feel safe when they are scared and frustrated. They will soon calm down. They are very empathic. Listen to them. They have no filter and might misunderstand us humans, but they do not lie; they just understand differently. They can see and feel your soul. They are here for a purpose. Not just autistic children but also all our children whom we call disabled are our special angels, and if one does choose you, you are very blessed. Never call these children disabled. They are special needs only because they need for all to see them, to understand them, to hear them. They are love. Can you teach and mainstream these children? Yes. Therefore, it is important to pay attention to them and learn from them. When a child is born deaf, you teach them sign language, correct? Learn their language.

Adults who have been mainstreamed and grounded solely to the earthly plane can reach the Akashic records and these dimensions through meditation by releasing their minds and their mental programming to connect to the universal consciousness, the Akashic records, and the realms of the universe. These realms of existence have been actively studied for one hundred years and even further back. Science has tried to find a physical way to prove or enter these other realities and dimensions. Quantum physics, the study of matter and energy at the subatomic level, has gone deep within the multiple dimensions and has discovered their existence. Quantum physicists have also discovered that the mind has access to these multi-dimensions through meditation and letting go of mental programming.

> Don't allow your belief to be suppressed by the intellect's demand for proof. Don't wait for proof. Believe and then allow the truth to manifest. (Emmanual, www.enlightenedbeings.com)

To understand any of this, to understand our children, we must shed ourselves of the programming that has been embedded into our humanness, let it go for the purposes of learning and understanding. These topics that I discuss in this book are to give you the whole picture, not to just tell the stories of children who remember their past lives. These stories are amazing and interesting, but you need more, and you need your own experience to fully understand. You need to understand that your child is not possessed or a product of something dark. They may not be making up stories. Their actions and words may be real past-life memories. Pay attention, and you may discover something amazing. You may view life and death from a different perspective. Your bond with your child will be even stronger. Children, especially newborns just entering this world, only know pure love and, their connections with whom some call their mothers and God in the spirit world in which they came as white light, full of love. They need, know and want that pure love.

Let go of mainstream attachments. Keep your mind open. Let them show you and remind you that we live in an infinite universe, which means that the thought of life has no beginning and ending. It is an earthly thought, for we never die, and we are never born. It is our physical body that experiences the beginning and ending of life and death. Who we are, our essences and our souls move on? Quiet your mind, for a child's mind in the early years has not been conditioned to accept human reality, which has been imposed on them through adults, religion, and cultural teachings. Let your child look into your eyes and tell you how much they missed you while waiting to come to Earth to be with you and, when they chose you, how they had watched and waited from the other side, excited for when they could begin the journey with you.

REINCARNATION AND THE
JOURNEY OF THE SOUL

Our lives may not be perfect, but the universe is.

REINCARNATION IS THE belief that one can return to the earthly, three-dimensional existence in a new physical form, whether it be human or animal. It is the belief that the form one takes in this new incarnation is determined by the behavior in the previous life, if the lessons were learned and what the contract or assignment consists of that was made before birth. Reincarnation has been one of the central tenets of many Eastern religions, such as Hinduism and Buddhism. They believe it is a path to purity and salvation. They believe that our soul lives through many lifetimes. The Egyptians, Greeks, Romans, and Aztecs all believed that there is a "transmigration of souls" from one body to the next after death. The common belief in all these religions is that reincarnation is the only option for the soul; the soul never dies, leaving reincarnation as the only option. Where it reincarnates and how it reincarnates is optional. I do believe this universe is vast and never-ending and that the soul is only a tiny speck within it. Many Christians have personal beliefs in reincarnation, but it is not in their doctrine. It is an overall belief of the Christian Church that reincarnation does not exist.

There have been many speculations outside of the Christian faith interpreting that John the Baptist had been reincarnated as the spirit of Elijah. This speculation stirs the pot a bit as to the belief and/or perception of reincarnation and forms a misinterpretation of the Christian belief. Plato once said, "When the soul enters into a physical body, it forgets where it came from and has no recollection of that previous experience." Since the days of Plato, there have been more discoveries, and although he was spot on, it has been discovered that all our past-life memories are stored in our soul and can be recalled.

Through children, we have discovered that there is memory after birth, and children at young ages tell us about it. So we do not forget our past lives and where we have been; this knowledge gets stored away in our soul consciousness/Akashic records. What we ourselves know in this lifetime about ourselves is very minimal. We cannot comprehend what gift we have or how powerful our souls really are. There is a vibrational imprint of all we have ever done and all the lives we have lived in our soul library, and we have access to it. Most people do not remember it because they have been conditioned and mainstreamed by our human and earthly culture and religious upbringing. They are not taught to look inside themselves for the answers, only up to God. We hide our inner selves, which are our souls. Most have no idea how powerful our human consciousness is and what our soul is capable of. We live on the surface and never go into our soul and connect with the lessons of the past. We ask our prospective God, "Why am I always getting hurt repeatedly? Why is my life this way? Why are my relationships not working, why do I feel this pain every day, and why can I not be happy?" Why? It is because we are not taught to go within the soul, past the level of emotion. When we say that we go deep and feel, most of the time, we are going deep into our emotions and not our whole soul. We let our emotions control our actions, whereas it is possible that if we actually close our eyes, meditate, and reach our souls, we would find our answers.

The veil that is between all dimensions and incarnations can be permeable, and the soul needs adjusting to the different worlds—from two dimensions to three dimensions as well as the opposite. It takes time for the soul and the human body to get used to the connection, although it is quicker coming into the body during birth than it is leaving the body at death. At birth, the soul is coming from a higher vibration and a place of all knowing, which makes it mentally abler to adjust more quickly to the surroundings and three-dimensional life than at the end of physical life, although the physical shock of being born is greater. When the soul decides to enter the baby, the body depends on the soul. I watched my granddaughter come in like a firecracker moments before she was born, and that is how she still is today—a firecracker. During the stage before birth, in the womb, the soul spends most of its time outside the mother, going in and out of the womb. There is not enough room yet for the soul to enter the body. There is too much electromagnetic interference from the mother's soul and things around it. The soul stays close until the time of birth, where it can make its attachment. Even after birth, the soul travels and visits other souls that it knows from the spirit world.

A child is born knowing that they are a soul with a body, and within those few short years, their soul is trying to reach out and give us messages that might help us heal or awaken us to our soul. Many times, the soul will return to the body of a relative because of karmic circumstances or to restore a broken life connection to finish the task that was not completed in the previous lifetime. The most popular question I have gotten asked about children reincarnating into the family is if it is possible for the soul of a young child who journeyed on to, soon after birth, return to the same parents as the soul of their next child. The creative force of existence is never separated from any form of living energy. Although children play a vital role in their regeneration of life and every soul has a motive for the events in which they came, could they choose to come back into the family they had left in a previous life? Yes, they could if the lessons were not completed. Sometimes the lesson is not for that soul but for the parents, so the need for reincarnation into the same parents is not necessary for the soul's journey. They may wait and choose another family member to reincarnate as because we journey with our same soul family. At a young age, they learn that every soul has a motive for the events in which they choose to participate. Babies show signs of their individuality as soon as they are born. That base personality grows with them and adds to their soul personality that they bring into their next lifetime, built on the experiences and the lessons they have learned.

SOUL MATES

Our first soul mate in our life is our mother.

S OUL MATES ARE also part of the agreement we make before we incarnate, but through human definition, soul mates have been romanticized as being "the one and only," the "true eternal love." "He is my soul mate for life." "She knows me so well. She can finish my sentences." "We are soul mates in love." This seems to be the popular definition of one's soul mate in today's language. A soul mate is someone whom you meet whom you feel an instant connection with, like you have known them before. You probably have. Through our human definition of soul mates, we are programmed to believe that this connection means you should have a romantic involvement. This is not so. A soul mate could be there to, at that time, be your teacher or help you through that period in life, to awaken you.

The philosopher Plato subscribed to and taught the idea that each of us only had one soul mate who was perfect for us, and if we found that soul mate, we would be complete. This theory has since been expanded. Through many years of study, it has changed the repertoire of the soul's connection and shows that it is more likely that we have a soul group, and with each lifetime we incarnate into, we discover new ones. So instead of one soul mate, we have many whom we have had deeper experiences with over many lifetimes. Having intense feelings of "I know you from somewhere" for a person you have never met is indicative of the soul connection from other lifetimes here in this lifetime. Some people have felt that strong, strong bond with someone and have mistaken that bond as a romantic bond, going deep into the intimacy of the relationship to find the relationship to be disastrous and, in some cases, missing something, thus making this relationship very confusing. The connection, as strong as it was, may have only been for another reason, such as to help awaken them or to fulfill a promise to help them in some way, but this was totally missed because our human definition says "romantic or forever." It is my belief that if we better understand what a soul mate is, it would greatly improve our lives because we would not be looking for that one divine love to move us forward on our journey. It is a fact that our soul is always looking for a connection. Our soul is energy that needs a ground. There could be more than one soul mate at a time. A soul mate can be a lover, a mother, a child, a best friend, and, yes, even a nemesis. To lose that soul mate is not a loss of opportunity to grow and evolve. The job of the soul mate may be complete, or they may leave and come back to complete another stage in the journey. Some soul mates whom we find, we have a connection with, but they might cause deep stress in our lives if we were to be in a relationship with them. So remember—a soul mate is not only a romantic partner. It indicates a deep connection and a knowing that you have known each other before. It is joy, sorrow, despair, growth, love, and much more. The connection is that of endless growth through lifetimes with another soul or group of souls. Major thorns in our life often come into our lives to be our soul mates or a part of a group of soul mates. They come along to give us their worst so we can learn something that we need to evolve. These soul mates have planned this and volunteered for this task in pre-birth planning. Our soul mate agreement is made in the astral plane and, when incarnated on earth, does not always work out as anticipated. Life happens, and choices and decisions have to be made and obstacles overcome. By the time we may meet them, earthly life could have taken its toll and habits and addictions formed. Life could have beaten them up. Their soul could have damage from what this earthly life has brought them.

When we meet our soul mates, our souls will know it. We will feel it deep, like we have met them before, and that little voice in our head would sound off. Everything in our body would send all sort of signals. Sometimes they are warning signs, but we ignore them because we are looking for the *one*, and we would be using our human brains, not our deep knowing. Many times, we see all the warning signs in the first few months of the relationship and refuse to acknowledge them. This is how we get sucked into toxic relationships. This comes from the misinterpretation of a soul mate. I can only tell you this: "If someone shows you who they are, believe them the first time." The soul will always show their true self for the good or the bad, especially early in the relationship. Both good and bad soul mates come into our lives to teach us lessons as well as be Earth angels. An Earth angel is someone from your soul family who comes into your life to act as a catalyst for change and helps you through those bad times of misjudgment.

Types of Soul Mates

Just as there are many soul mates in our lives, there are many types of soul mates who come into our lives:

Soul Teachers: They are healers and mentors. They are those who teach you by challenging you, who teach you value and how to think for yourself. They are incredibly special, and your relationships with them are very sacred.

Soul Contracts: These are people who come into our lives, whom we made contracts with before incarnation on a soul level and whom we meet to learn and accomplish certain things in this lifetime.

Soul Crossings: They come into your life, but the timing is not right, or the circumstances are not right. Maybe they are married, or you're in a position where a relationship is forbidden or the age difference is not workable. Although they may not be able to have a long-term relationship with you, they may share a bonding experience and an awakening with you.

Past-Life Soul Mates: Past-life soul mates come into our lives looking to heal and do better this time around.

Soul Ties: They are the ties that bond and are here to inspire you, encourage you. They are our feel-good soul mates. They could be persons or animals.

Karmic Souls: These "wrecking-ball soul mates" come into our lives as agents of change to help make it easier to journey through positive, negative, or neutral interactions and give us opportunities to improve our karma.

Soul Families and Soul Groups: These are family members and people working toward common goals. Sometimes one soul will reincarnate to try to help heal something in the family line, like a pattern of addiction and abuse.

Kindred Spirits: They are not always soul mates, but they really understand you and may share some common things with you, such as spiritual beliefs and viewpoints. They have many similar life experiences. You may even finish each other's sentences.

Twin Flames: I have heard this from people all the time among best friends, but a twin flame is one soul that is split into two bodies. They are not ultimately here for romantic relationships. Twin flames can be of the opposite gender or of the same gender. They do not always come here to connect because they are split in the astral plane to experience and learn different lessons, but when they do come, they do so to help you achieve more enlightenment into your life. They are here to heal you in unique and powerful ways, challenge you, and teach you with love. When they come together in the spirit world after their earthly journey, they come together as one soul that has experienced different lessons to help evolve more quickly.

Soul Partners: These include best friends and in-laws. They may raise children together or be business partners. They can be someone intimate or whom you may know all your life. They could be siblings. They support you in this life emotionally and professionally, and they are here to help you accomplish and experience what your soul planned to do on Earth.

Romantic Soul Mates: Romantic soul mates tend to tap-dance on your biggest wounds or challenge you in uncomfortable ways. When they enter a relationship, they also enter the earth school together and share lessons.

Karma is not judgment. It is consequences.
We are the ones responsible.

— Timber Hawkeye, *Buddhist Boot Camp*

KARMA

WHEN SOMETHING BAD happens by the hands of another person, we tend to say, "He/she will get their karma." Karma is looked at as a punishment for a wrong action, and we are comforted by the thought of some kind of justice of bad deeds that will soon come full circle, like an eye for an eye or a tooth for a tooth. People believe that God or some higher power will intercede and make it all better when justice does not seem to be good enough; to some, karma is an extra slap in the face to remind the person whom they messed with. This meaning gives us what we need when we feel hurt and devastated, and this idea seems to be the only control we feel that we have in the given situation, making this definition of karma satisfying. We then look past the deeper and spiritual meaning.

> How people treat you is their karma.
> How you react is yours. (Dr. Wayne Dyer)

Many cultures and beliefs view karma as an especially important part of their cultural or religious structure. Newton's third law of motion implies that nothing that does not act in accordance with the law of cause and effect exists. "For every action, thought, or feeling, there is an equal and opposite reaction" (www.ck-12.org/physics, November 1, 2012). This is Newton's theory, but in the case of karma, his theory gets lost in the wording and the perceivable meaning that actions and reactions are immediate. Karma is about what the person has done (past action), is doing (present action), and will do (future action), making them measurable and assessed. The main conception is that you get what you give, good or bad, and are accountable for all of it. Although Newman's theory is based on immediate action, its idea of cause and effect explains karma.

The Sanskrit meaning of "action," "effect," or "fate" with a spiritual meaning implies cause and effect. Whatever you send out returns to you, positive or negative. You reap what you sow and do unto others what you want done unto you. All describe karma, and all state that there are consequences for all actions; your intent plus your actions will and do dictate your future. Each action dictates a corresponding action. It will also have a rippling effect on your future lives. Each soul that reincarnates has karma. It is part of the reason we are here, part of our lesson, or part of our teaching others. Our children have memories of this. The Bible says, "We are all born sinners." I guess if the only karma that we have to fulfill is bad karma, then this statement could hold truth, but our karmic debt is part of our curriculum in this earth school. There are things we have learned in our past lives that we are here to teach others, and there are things in our curriculum that we need to learn. If we do not learn them, we have to take the course all over again. Some misunderstand what the course is about. For example, if you were a mean and selfish person who hurt a lot of people in your past life, then your course lesson would be about giving to others, healing the injured, maybe forgiveness. Karma is not about judgment or revenge; it is about learning, enlightenment, evolving, getting closer to oneness. When we do not learn these lessons, we will repeat them.

Karma is energy, so it can be manipulated and changed. Where there is negative, there is also positive, so to say that karma is only negative energy is a misunderstood thought.

Karma is imprinted on the soul who had created the energy, not by the one who had received the energy. We cannot be given karma. Karma is self-inflicted, self-learned. Your humanness created the action or thought on a human level. Karma is not a judgment that God or the universe put upon you or a punishment. I hear all the time, "I must have done something so bad in my past life for this to be going on in my life now." No. Your humanness created that situation. Your decisions and free will did this. Karma is a lesson at the soul level, the "contract" that keeps our souls evolving and helps us rise in consciousness. As the soul evolves and develops our consciousness, we grow and start to see things differently. It is on us to do nice and loving things, but the important part of the lesson is in the true meaning of the soul. In other words, it is not enough to be nice to someone today so you can "wipe away" bad karma or reap some "reward points." That does not count. It is being genuine on a soul level. When we grow and start to see things differently, we will start to see the connection and the energy patterns that are born within ourselves and the universe. We will see it in the eyes and energy of our children, and upon their arrival, we will be able to recognize their lessons and what they must teach us.

Karma gives us a purpose to reincarnate and gives us the lesson we must work on and share with others in this lifetime. We are all here on Earth as students to learn these important lessons and should not interfere with other humans' karmic lessons by telling them what to do or forcing them to something they do not want to do. If we listen to our children from the beginning of life, could it be possible for us to open those doors early in their lives to achieve some of the lessons that they are here to learn so they can advance and evolve in their next lifetime? Is that the true job of the parents? This action may also change the course of others' lives as well. Karma is an ongoing process that occurs every day in our earthly humanness and continues into our next lifetime until we reach oneness or, as some might believe, until we reach God. It is important to remember that karma dictates that the circle of life will continue. It is an essential part of life, death, and rebirth. My next story is a good example of reincarnation, soul mates, and karma. This is surely the circle of life.

WHEN PAST LIVES ARE IGNORED: "REMEMBER, MOMMY?"

RAVEN WAS TWENTY-THREE when she had met Cole. Cole was the original bad boy and was what every woman referred to as "tall, dark, and handsome"—nicely built, with dark hair, brown eyes, and a tanned beach body. Raven was a sassy blonde with green eyes and looking for adventure. Raven and Cole hit it off. It was not long before they were happy in love and inseparable. Cole was the romantic kind of guy and would often do sweet things for Raven, like stop in the middle of a back road on a beautiful summer day to pick a beautiful flower for her just to say, "I love you." They went to parties and were the ideal couple. They lived happily and on the edge, and it was perfect.

As time went on, Raven found out that she was pregnant and, eight and a half months later, gave birth to a beautiful baby girl. They named her Amber Rose, which was very fitting for her because her eyes, as she grew older, had specks of amber in them, and her cheeks had the slightest tint of rose. She had her daddy's dark hair, soft with the slightest of curls. She was their pride and joy. After Amber's birth, things got tough. Money was tight, and Amber was a little premature and had to stay in the hospital a few more days than usual for special care, which made the hospital bill skyrocket. They stopped going to parties, and adult life began. As money got tight and life set in, Raven and Cole started fighting, and many times, Cole would get so upset, he would leave and go down the street to the nearest pub to cool down and think of ways to make things better. He loved Raven and Amber, but things were hard.

As months went by, Raven and Cole decided to go their separate ways, and Raven was left to take care of Amber. Raising a child on her own was a struggle, like it is for most single parents, but Amber was a challenge because she often suffered from night terrors. She would wake up in the middle of the night, slashing around like she was running from something and screaming, "Mama! Mama! Help!" Raven would have to pick Amber up and soothe her until she fell asleep. That would take hours, and she had to be in for work at the glass company at five o'clock every morning, Monday through Friday and most Saturdays, if she was lucky enough to pick up more hours. Her job was forty-five minutes away, so Raven had to be up by 3:00 a.m. to leave by 4:00 a.m. In the early eighties, the idea of past lives was still hidden in the closet for fear of deep ridicule, and to say that your child had night terrors would lead to only two conclusions: either your child was possessed and had mental issues because of it, or your child was abused and tormented. Neither explanation was the truth. This went on for years, and as Amber got older, she started to get more afraid.

One day Amber said to her mother, "Mommy, why didn't you come save me? You promised you would not let anyone hurt me."

Raven was startled by the words her little girl was saying. She got down on her knees, looked into Amber's eyes, and said, "Oh no, honey. You're my sunshine. You must have had a bad dream. I love you. I would not let anything happen to you, my sweet girl."

Amber looked at her mommy and said, "That's what you always said, but when you were my mommy before, you did, they took me, and I died."

Raven was speechless; she did not know what to say. Amber ran off and went to play with her toys. The next few days, Amber slept through the night with no terrors, and she stayed in her bed, with only a hall light on all night, but Raven was puzzled, and that was all she could think about. This all came out of nowhere, without a single clue as to why or what Amber was talking about. *How could my daughter ever think that way about me?* Raven thought. *And what did she mean by "when you were my mommy before"?* Trying to find answers in a world of no cell phones and internet would leave you racking your brain for answers at 2:00 a.m. The 1980s was a time of leg warmers, crazy hairstyles, and a whole other language than today. Modern paganism was just rising in the publishing world, but so did what they called "the Satanic Panic." American culture was defined by proud political and social conservatism. Past-life regression was a new concept being brought to the mainstream. *New Age Spiritual Evolution of the 1980s with Dr. Brian Weiss with Many Lives, Many Masters* (1988, Touchstone Publishing), *The Children That Time Forgot* by Peter and Mary Harrison, first published as *Life before Birth* (1983, Futura Publications), and *Eye of the Centaur: A Visionary Guide to Past Lives* by Barbara Hand Clow (1989, Bear & Company Publishing) were some of the first books to come out for believers in past lives. From a young age, Raven found knowledge in books and would walk a few blocks to read and research topics she was interested in or go on adventures in some magical faraway land in a novel. She could not afford books of her own, so the library and New Age shops were where she had to find her knowledge and interests. It was also at that time when Raven chose to meet others of her beliefs. Once every couple of weeks, on a Tuesday night, they would meet at the local coffee shop and discuss topics they had an interest in, and she could network in the pagan community. Raven decided that since she trusted in her pagan friends, she would ask their opinions on what happened with her daughter, Amber. She thought that maybe they could help her make sense of it all. Willow, one of the group's members, said she felt that it could be a past-life thing and that her daughter remembered her past life with Raven and her death. They suggested that Raven find a regressionist and do a past-life regression, and then Raven could find out what happened and be able to help Amber heal.

When Raven called and set up a consultation, I could feel her apprehension, and I knew this was important to her. There was a desperation in her voice that I had not heard before. I set her up with me the next day. When Raven had arrived at the appointment, she had Amber with her so that I would have an opportunity to talk to Amber before Raven had her regression. I had set up a play area for Amber so she had something to play with to help her relax. Amber and I would talk, and I would just ask some open questions to trigger her response. The first part of the interview would be with Raven. She gave me some background information, starting from when Amber was born.

When she got to the part where Amber had asked her mommy why she did not come save her, Raven said, "I do not know why my little girl would say that to me. It was like she was talking to someone else, but she was looking at me."

"I said that, Mommy, because you did not save me. You let them take me, and I died. You promised!" Amber yelled. "You promised, Mommy!"

Amber stomped, threw herself to the ground, pulled her legs up tight to her chest, covered her face with her hands, and cried. Raven was devastated. She did not know how to react. Amber had never done this in public.

I told Raven, "Just go over and hug her. Let her know you love her."

Raven did as I had asked, and Amber accepted her mother's hug. She kissed her mother's cheek and went back to play like nothing had happened.

Raven looked at me with fear and confusion. "I do not know where this comes from. I thought maybe she was having a dream she was remembering. And then my friend Willow said it could be from a past life we shared. I took Amber to her doctor, and his explanation was nightmares or night terrors that she is remembering, and it keeps coming back at times. Could this be what is happening?"

I said, "It is apparent to me that Amber has a past-life memory that she shares with you. She is at that age, and now is verbalizing the memory. What I would like to do is do a past-life regression with you and see what you connect with. I would also like to give you the knowledge and a second option, which is to let this ride out. Eventually, in a few years, Amber's memories will fade, and if later in life, she wants to revisit this and have a regression herself, it will be healing for her."

Raven wanted to know more and agreed to the regression. Raven confided that ever since her daughter had first said something, she thought about nothing else. Raven wanted to understand. She wanted to know if a past life was possible and if it was possible that she and Amber had lived another life together. She also wanted to help Amber now since she could see how this was hurting Amber emotionally, and Raven was afraid of the adverse effects on her daughter and on their relationship. Now that Raven had the knowledge of past lives, as she looked back, she could see the signs and the patterns.

Raven was eager to get started right away, so I gave her some things to work on to get ready for the regression, some information on the benefits of a regression, and some background on past lives. The session was two hours, and Raven did not have any problems reaching her past life with her now present daughter. We discovered two recent lives that she had shared with Amber. In one life, Amber and Raven were brother and sister. They both died when their house had burned down in their village. The second life was when Raven was the mother of Amber. In this lifetime, we discovered that Emily (not her real name in the regression) had been forcibly kidnapped from her mother by strange masked men while her mother was left for dead. I remind you that this is Raven's memory, so she would only see what she went through or was present for (Rosemary was her name in the past life). When Rosemary woke up, days had gone by, and her daughter was nowhere to be found. She called for her, searched for her, and put "Have you seen my daughter?" posters up. She searched and searched until she died. Rosemary's last moments with her daughter were when two masked men had come and abducted her daughter as she screamed for her mother to help her.

Rosemary tried to get her daughter from the masked men, yelling, "I will find you and get you back, and they will pay!" and then was hit from the back and left for dead.

I brought Raven back out of the regression and to this period and gave her a moment to process and regroup. Raven had never done this before; nor did she ever think that this was a possibility.

She looked at me, smiled with tears in her eyes, and said, "I found her. I found Emily here, in this lifetime." Then she sat back with complete joy and added, "No, Emily found me."

Raven called me just to keep in touch and told me that she had gone home, looked into her daughter's eyes, and said, "Emily, it is okay now. You found me." She hugged her tight and said, "Thank you," to her daughter.

All throughout Amber's childhood, Raven and Amber were close, and Amber never again had that past-life memory. As Amber reached puberty, things started to change, and Amber became defiant and resentful of Raven. When Raven tried to discipline Amber for the things she did, Amber would rebelliously snap back at her, telling her that she had no idea about anything that Amber was going through. Raven tried to teach her. She tried to help her through those tough years, but Amber would snap at Raven and say hurtful things to her. She again told Raven that she was never there for her. Raven knew that much of this anxiety was coming from the past life of Emily, the emotions that she never let go and that were hidden deep and triggered by puberty. This kept going on long after Amber had children of her own. Amber and Raven's relationship was on and off. Raven hoped that it would change.

Raven talked to Amber about a regression and reminded her of the past life, and Amber just shrugged it off. It was not something she wholeheartedly believed in. Raven accepted that because she knew that we all have free will, and although it hurt her emotionally, she lived her life out, being a loving grandmother to her grandchildren, and hoped that one day they would know the truth of who Raven was. Raven journeyed on to her next lifetime, knowing she had fulfilled her lessons here and she would meet Amber again in another lifetime.

The thought here is that as our souls are here to work out things that might need to be finished in the past life, learn the lessons and fulfill contracts made in the in-between, we do need to recognize them to evolve, for the purpose of life is love. We still have free will to make our own paths, to learn these lessons, or we will have to repeat them to evolve to oneness. Raven showed unconditional love no matter what Amber had put in her path. She was there beside Amber in good times and rough times, always trying to lift her up, but Amber could only go as high as the nearest cloud. She could never see past the cloud. I am hopeful that Amber learned her lessons of gratitude, love, and forgiveness after her mother had journeyed on. Amber and Raven were soul mates that made this contract to learn this lesson and to complete their unfinished business, and they each had karma all throughout a past life. Amber never healed her relationship with her mother. Amber, according to karmic law, will be learning this lesson in the next life.

Divine love—a kind of love that never varies and never changes, a state of being in which there [are] no opposites. It is pure oneness.

— Dr. Wayne Dyer, *Memories from Heaven*

OPHELIA AND BENJAMIN

OPHELIA & Benjamin

And Then We Met Again......

B ENJAMIN WAS THREE years old when Ophelia was born. During the time his aunt was pregnant with Ophelia, Benjamin had a connection with her. He knew that he knew Ophelia before he was born into this earthly life. He remembered Ophelia from another life when she was his mother. Her name was Delilah, and they called her by her nickname, Peachy Pie, because when asked how her day was, she would say, "Just peachy." Peachy Pie also happened to be the nickname of Benjamin's grandmother who had journeyed on before Benjamin was born.

During the time Ophelia was still in the womb, Benjamin would go up to her mommy, push her belly button, and say, "Tootles, Peachy Pie." When asked who was in the belly, Benjamin would say, "Peachy Pie is in there."

"Who is Peachy Pie?" his nanny would ask.

Benjamin would say, "That's my mommy." Benjamin would cup his little hand and wave at the pregnant belly. "Come out soon, Peachy Pie."

As it got closer to the arrival of Ophelia, Benjamin got excited. "Nanny, when is she coming? I am waiting and waiting."

"Soon," his nanny would say.

Children at that age have no sense of time, and babies traveling here have no time specified. So "soon" was the best answer, but "soon" meant to Benjamin "now." When Ophelia was born, she was a week late but healthy and ready to take on the world. It is amazing, seeing a newborn when they are first born. Like I have mentioned in my other books, I have experienced with my grandchildren the moment of life and the moment of entry into this earthly world. When you are open to this knowledge, you can see and experience the jarring paroxysm of birth, the awakening and joining and the final union of the soul and body and its new connection to this earthly world. It enters with blinding hospital lights and having to breathe air and feel physical touch for the first time. They look around as if they are coming out of a deep sleep and wonder where they were, constantly looking and recognizing.

It was a few weeks before Benjamin got to meet Ophelia. When the day came, Benjamin was excited, so when he got to his nanny's house, where Ophelia and her mommy and daddy were visiting, he ran right in the house.

"Nanny, where is the baby? Where is Peachy Pie?"

He looked in the living room, and there was the bassinette with a little baby in it. Benjamin stopped at the entrance and just looked at where the baby lay. She was crying, and everyone was trying to soothe her.

He turned around and walked back to his nanny, pouting. "Nanny, the baby does not like me. She is crying."

"Sure, she does, Benjamin. She is probably hungry." His nanny picked him up and brought him in to meet Ophelia.

The moment she saw Benjamin, she stopped crying and locked eyes on him, and they both just gazed at each other. Everyone was still as they watched and felt the connection between these two. Benjamin broke the gaze and turned around to play with his toys. As he did, Ophelia started to cry again. Benjamin got up and went back to Ophelia, and she stopped crying and focused again on Benjamin.

When Benjamin had to go home, he went to Ophelia and said, "Goodbye, Peachy Pie."

As Ophelia's mother one day was changing her diaper and giving her a bath, she noticed a mark just above the ankle, a little dot, like someone had marked her with a marker. It was just a little dot on her porcelain skin. When she was done with Ophelia's bath, she brought her out to her mother-in-law, who reacted with such joy.

"It worked!" she said with excitement and continued to explain.

She had read that if you mark someone you love when they die, when a child is born, you can identify them by the marking. So when her mother-in-law, Delilah, had passed away, she quickly took a Sharpie marker and put a dot on her ankle.

"I had looked for it the day Ophelia was born but did not see it, but there it is, right where I marked her, the same ankle, same spot, and now that Ophelia has grown into her skin, we can see it," she explained. "This explains why Benjamin calls her Peachy Pie—because he sees who she is. He knows. If he is Steve, her son, he knows and has known." This was confirmed by Ophelia, when she began to talk one word at a time.

Benjamin spent a lot of time with Ophelia because while their mothers went to work, their nanny would watch them. One day Benjamin seemed a little sad.

His nanny asked him what was bothering him, and he said, "My mommy is not big like you."

Thinking that he was speaking of his own mommy, his nanny said, "That is because your mommy is my daughter."

Benjamin looked at her, puzzled. "No, my mommy, Peachy Pie. She is not growing to be big like you."

"She will, Benjamin. She will."

As Ophelia got older, she would get all excited when Benjamin came to see her and would always kick and scream until she got a hug. When she started to talk, she started calling him not by Benjamin but by the name he had in his previous life: Steve.

She would say, "Hey, Steedie." she couldn't say Stevie very well.

Steve had died traumatically four years before Benjamin was born and Steve's mother, Delilah, died four years after her son Steven had died, and she used to call him Stevie. Whenever Ophelia saw Benjamin, she would get all excited and yell for Stevie and crawl or run to him for a hug and kiss on the cheek. Everyone tried to tell her his name was Benjamin, but she would not have it. During play, Benjamin and Ophelia would have conversations. It would be more like Benjamin would talk, and Ophelia would have babbles and hand gestures because she was only speaking a few words and babbling seemed to be the understood language. One instance, Benjamin was playing with his cars, and Ophelia was in her seat, watching her show on TV and eating her breakfast.

Benjamin went up to Ophelia and said to her, "I remember when you had to tell the doctors to let me go and I died. I'm sorry I made you cry. I am sorry they got mad. I was ready to go. I'm sorry." Then he kissed Ophelia.

The moment his nanny had heard what he was saying, it felt like everything went silent and time stopped just for a second. Ophelia was still and quiet as she looked at him while he talked. It seemed like she had understood everything he was saying. It was at that moment that Stevie forgave his mother for having to make that hard decision that no one else could make and let him journey on. His nanny's life changed that day, and it may have healed a little piece of her heart as well.

Today Ophelia still gets excited when she sees Benjamin, and she still calls him Stevie and pounds her fist when they try and tell her differently. Only time will tell how long these two will have this past-life memory, but for now, every once in a while, you could hear Benjamin say, "Remember when I was big?"

This story and the next one both present some kind of birthmark or defect from a past life. Ophelia's was put there by her grandmother in this lifetime at the time of her previous life's passing to possibly identify her if she was reincarnated into this lifetime. Many Middle Eastern cultures did that in the past. Some did it to identify criminals or enemies so that if they reincarnated, they would be able to identify them immediately as the enemy.

This brought me to think deeper and make sense of this possibility of why they manifest in the next lifetime. Birthmarks are past-life scars and can provide powerful evidence of a past life when matched with a wound from a past life. They usually correspond with a past-life trauma. The trauma imprints on the soul. When the period between death in their past life and birth in their present life is short, the wound would not have enough time to heal the imprint and damage on the soul prior to rebirth. Another reason for the birthmark to manifest in the present lifetime is that the soul needs to reconnect with his or her past wounds and traumas so that the soul can be healed from the trauma and set free.

Just an angry girl inside,
Shattered from the core,
She put her feelings aside,
But suddenly, the tears pour.
She tried to keep her head up,
But she wasn't the least bit okay.
You could catch her tears in a cup.
She felt the world should pay.
This girl is broken.
This girl is not together.
This girl was smokin'.
Would she make it in this weather?

— Lizzy Travis

OWL PHOENIX: TWO LIVES REMEMBERED

Listen. The wisdom of the universe speaks in whispers. Do you hear it?

T HERE IS SO much research and stories today by prominent doctors in psychology, scientists, and many other authors who have been fascinated by the phenomenon of children remembering past lives. I have often wondered if this has always been talked about or if children, when they were in the age group of two to seven years old, were ignored and swept to the side or whether they were just disregarded because, as the saying goes, "children have such good imagination." I vividly remember when we called those years "the formative years." Could that mean the same for us as well?

Many authors such as Carol Bowman, Ian Stevenson, Jim B. Tucker, and Tom Schroder have spent many years of research on children's past-life memories. It has only been in the past decade that this topic has made it to the forefront and that more and more information that supports this phenomenon is coming out. Researching for this book, I'd had many people come forward, wanting to tell their stories, looking for validation and answers. My advice to them has always been "If you give your child permission to talk about when they were big, they will feel safe and not fear to communicate." Each new life brings in new messages and stories that awaken and astonish us, each story more paramount than the last. Why now? Are we just hearing and seeing it now, or has this been happening all along and we have been dismissing it? Is this our universal awakening for those who are open to hear its whispers? I believe it is all a part of the process of life and has always been right there among the joyous celebrations of birth but gets grounded in the dogma of our earthly renditions of life. We feel that we need to follow a checklist of what life is supposed to be. We end up leading with a blind eye to the true freedom and spiritual wonders that exist in life. Children of young ages such as these know no lies. They have not mastered that concept. They do not even know what an imagination is yet. So when two-year olds start speaking of things, people, and places they have not had the time to learn about, why are we not listening? It is not my belief that only a select few remember. I believe all children do. Either they just do not speak of it or we are not hearing it—and then it fades. Some memories even become the monsters under their beds in their dreams later in life. Some memories are from more than one past life—like in the story of Owl Phoenix.

Phoenix was an adorable little blond boy with big eyes that lit up and an impish smile that let you know he was on a mission. Phoenix was born to a family who lived in the countryside of Pennsylvania. He had five other siblings to share his life with. He chose to be born in a family with many conflicts but close bonds. When I had an interview with this family, the mother had told me that she thought that her son was a reincarnation of her step-uncle Brian, whom she was remarkably close to and who had died a few years before Phoenix was born. Her uncle's death left much controversy within the family and bad blood that shattered them. For many years after, most of the family did not speak. Her uncle lived his life in the fast lane, living life to the fullest and as close to the edge as he could possibly go. His motto in life was "You do you, and I do me. If we like each other, we will be friends forever. If not, that's okay too." Brian lived the life of an entrepreneur, and it took up much of his time. Family time was lived in minutes, but that was Brian, always living and always smiling.

His death was tragic and shook the family to the core. When he passed away tragically, it was like a bomb had gone off in this family. Secrets that were locked away were no longer secrets, the things Brian had kept in the closet of his life came out, and family judgment started everywhere. The little thing about judgment is that people forget that there is more than one side to the story, and dead or alive, Brian was going to tell it. Brian lay in a coma, on a respirator, for two months when they decided that it was time to make that choice, and within twenty-four hours of having to turn off the machines, Brian had passed. Brian was an organ donor, so the immediate family hoped that maybe Brian's organs would be able to save someone else's life. The funeral was held, and then everyone went their separate ways. Each family group stayed in their respective corners. This close family now seemed like they were the Hatfields and the McCoys.

When Owl Phoenix was born, he came in running. He did not scream and cry like most babies do. He came into this world squinting and wiggling away, as if he had been sleeping and someone just woke him up. When he opened his eyes, they opened big as he wiggled around to see what was going on and where he was. He was an exceptionally good baby and adjusted to earthly life very well. After a few months, it was time for his mother to return to work, so like in most close-knit families, Phoenix's grandmother took care of him while his parents went to work. Phoenix loved being at his grandmother's and would put up a fuss when it was time for him to go home. For a while, his mother and grandmother thought that the fussing was just that his grandmother had nobody but her and Grandpa at home and that it was quiet and cozy. His home was full of normal sibling rivalry and joyous laughter, and sometimes it was outright loud because of all the hustle and bustle, but as Phoenix grew up, they started to notice more and more the connection he had with his grandparents.

When Phoenix started to talk one day, out of the blue, he looked at his grandfather, smiled, and said, clearer than day, "Bub." Bub was a nickname only Brian called him. His grandfather had not heard that nickname in years. He leaned down and picked up Phoenix for a hug. When his grandfather picked him up, he noticed the scar on the right side of Phoenix's head, above his forehead, in the same spot where Brian's head injury was from his accident that took his life six years before. Excitement flashed though his grandfather as the thought of Brian being reborn as Phoenix came to mind. He knew it was the essence of Brian, his only brother, in his heart.

He felt it, but he had to ask, "Did Phoenix somehow have an injury that we did not know about?"

He pointed to the scar on his head. Aubrey, Phoenix's grandmother, lightly pushed away some hair to reveal the scar. She was puzzled because an injury to leave that kind of scar would have been noticeable. Clearly, their daughter would have said something, and they would have seen the bandages. They were a close family, and Aubrey had been their childcare provider since before Phoenix was born; if there was an injury that serious, she would know about it. Their minds got drawn back to the last time they had seen Brian in the hospital bed. Brian had a head injury from the crash in that very same spot.

"Brian?" his grandfather said as he looked back at Phoenix and turned his head to look into his eyes.

Phoenix smiled and said again, "Bub."

He wrapped his arms around his grandfather's neck, kissed him on the cheek, turned to look deep into his grandfather's eyes, wrapped his arms around him again, and hugged him tight like it was the first time he had ever hugged his grandfather. The energy and joy of that moment brought tears to his grandfather's eyes.

Phoenix, like Brian, loved to be in the kitchen and always wanted to help cook or taste the food that his grandparents were cooking. Brian was the owner of a restaurant chain when he had died; cooking was his passion. Phoenix made it his mission to make sure that the dishwasher had the pod in the dispenser and was ready to go. If his grandmother or grandfather tried to wash the dishes by hand, Phoenix would point his finger and announce sternly that they needed to "sterile" (big word for three and a half years old, meaning "sterilize") the dishes.

When spring hit the year of Phoenix's almost third birthday, Phoenix got sick and had to go to the doctor to get checked out. During that time, they had discovered scar tissue on the inside of his throat.

The doctor asked, "Has Phoenix ever had tubes down his throat?"

His mother replied, puzzled, "No. Why would you ask that?"

"Because the film we took of his throat shows that he has scar tissue that would indicate that he had tubes down his throat."

There was no explanation that this lifetime could provide. While talking with his grandfather, they discovered that Brian had been on life support for almost two months before he passed away. That would have left scars because of the amount of time the tube was left in.

Second Life Remembered

One day Phoenix and his grandmother, Aubrey, were in the kitchen, preparing dinner. His grandmother would put the dry ingredients in little bowls and let Phoenix add them to the recipe for that day.

Phoenix looked at Aubrey and said, "Grandma, who is Lisa?"

Aubrey thought that maybe Phoenix had heard them talking about Lisa at times and wanted to know who she was. "Lisa is Grandpa's mommy, who is in heaven. She went to heaven before you were born."

"I met her before I was born." Phoenix was using his words. "She was my big sister. When we did makeup."

Aubrey smiled and said, "You mean the last time before you were born?"

Phoenix said, "Before I was big, yesterday, when I was small and big and Evy was bigger". Evy is Phoenix's big sister in this lifetime he recognized from his past life," I had a baby in my tummy." Evy got sick and died. I was sad. Grandma, do you have a mirror you hold in your hand? Like Evy?"

"No, Phoenix, but my mommy had one," Aubrey said.

"I like them," Phoenix said with a nod and a smile. "Shhh. Do not tell Mommy. She said I am a boy!"

"Okay," said Aubrey. "That will be our secret."

That was the first time Phoenix had talked about a life before his previous life. Phoenix had remembered two lifetimes very clearly, and in each lifetime, he was of a different gender. In each lifetime, we found, Phoenix was not held back by culture or religious beliefs as some cultures or beliefs dictate that a soul reincarnates only in the same sex that it was in in the prior lifetime. If you were born a boy, you would always be a boy. Phoenix's story also shows that your soul sees life as one continuous journey as Phoenix remembered two lifetimes, his first lifetime being the most recent.

I live in accordance
with nature and therefore
never go against the way of things.

— Dr. Wayne Dyer, *Living the Wisdom of the Tao*

LIVING IN TWO WORLDS

I AM SURE THAT you have read books or seen movies where the person has talked about living in two worlds. The concept, for most, is something that they cannot wrap their heads around or have never had serious thoughts about. If you are a spiritual person who is not grounded to the doctrine of the church, you may understand with clarity what I mean. I have been what is called a walker between both worlds, in and out, all my life. I believed as a young child locked in a closet that my abilities had given me the ability to survive. I could astral-travel outside of the small area, go in and out of this earthly dimension, and receive solace and help from my spirit family. These are some of the reasons now that I can do the things I do and have done for all the years of my life here. Some people who are closest to me will often joke with me and say, "You're always living on the edge," or when I seem to be in my zone, they will say things like "Earth to Trish. Come back, Trish." I laugh and find it very endearing because I know this is how they understand and that surely, there is no malice in their words. When I do come fully back, they welcome me with excitement, wanting to know where I have been and what messages I bring back.

To make it clear, I am not one of those people you see in movies who all of a sudden go into this trance. Their eyeballs flip into their head, and they go limp. Then all of a sudden, they awaken with a jolt, and their eyes pop open. Sorry to disappoint you, but for me, it is much subtler than that, and most people who do not know me do not even notice. To me, this ability is as normal as breathing. We are born into this earthly world, in tune with all our senses, barely able to see the world around us. We use touch, smell, hearing, and feeling to identify the energy and the people in this world we were just born into. Infants are born with barely any eyesight but know when someone outside of the normal everyday life holds them or if they are in the room just by using all their senses and feeling the energy in the room. This is how we adapt to this world; this is how we are born. Infants and toddlers look into your eyes for answers and can feel your anxiety when you're stressed. They awaken when you tiptoe in a room, when your energy gets too close, or when your smell brushes their nose. An infant is soothed by the smell of a mother's shirt when given to them when she is away. Then there are those times when they just stare into space, and it almost appears as if they have vacated the room and are in a trance. We say, "Hey, sweetheart. Hello? Are you there? Where did you go? Come back!" and then "Oh, there you are. Welcome back" as they slightly jolt back into reality. Sometimes it can be awfully boring as the little human's body develops and the soul just zips around from this world to the world it came from to commune with other souls. Soon enough, our parents start getting involved in our development, and things start to change. At the most crucial years of my life, when a toddler is like a sponge and learns the most from its outside world and the family that surrounds them, I was taken away from my mother and put into foster care. I never stayed in one place long enough to be mainstreamed, so my abilities stayed intact. I was labeled as a disturbed child because of my abilities and the things that I remembered. Not too many families could deal with that—and addressing the situation? Well, that was too much for them to deal with as well. I told stories of a life before this life as a merchant around the time of the Boston Tea Party. I always wanted to go home, I would say, and home was not with my mother. I talked about going home, and home was my special place, where light music played all the time and different colored bubbles would float around, which I knew to be souls. They spoke to one another, and if you wanted to be somewhere, you just communicated it, and you were there. Speaking was not through mouth and voice; it was through thought, telepathically. I talked about this brightness and this peaceful feeling all the time. They thought I was very imaginative for a four-year-old.

I always felt like I did not belong here. No one understood my abilities. No one understood that loud noises hurt me. Large crowds and chaotic energy made me an emotional roller coaster, as did going into stores, feeling the energy of the people, and hearing the hum of the lights—seeing spirits and hearing people's thoughts. To them, I was disturbed. To them, I was different, different in ways they did not understand. Frustration filled my mind, and anger filled my heart at times when the knowing I had was not taken to heart. "Listen to me," I would say, but they could not. To them, I was belligerent. They put labels on me. They feared me, so I was abandoned in a hospital. I was too different for them to handle. I was with one family for two months before they called the case worker and told them I was not a good fit for them. The connection was not there. Their energy told me, and I just knew. So I packed up my toys before the state worker came and got me. When she arrived, I picked up my box of toys and went to the car.

"I want to go home. It is a lot different from here. Everything is happy, and everyone loves everyone. It does not feel like that here." I did not cry. I just went to the next home.

Today they would have called me autistic or said that I had ADHD or some other label that medicine or science could come up with. What they do not know is I am neither. I am an empath, a psychic. I can talk to the dead, and they can talk to me. I am tuned into all my senses and embrace all my abilities and have claimed myself as who I am. I have always accepted myself. I am not the only one like me. There are other children, some of whom were in foster care and some of whom remained within their birth family and have had the same experiences and managed to keep their memories of the life before and the in-between, as just a soul, as I have. To make it simpler, we are all born this way. Those of us who were not mainstreamed had invisible friends that our parents thought were cute, and we were labeled as having a good imagination with our "imaginary friends." Some parents fear that their children are talking to spirits. These children are born with a higher vibration and sensitivity, and other souls/spirits can see and feel that ability within the child. This goes for all humans who hold onto this ability, such as mediums. The soul/spirit will gravitate to the vibration of the child, maybe to give a message to someone, but they are generally harmless. Some want to play. I used to play with a little boy at a hotel whose family had been burned in a fire nearby.

Because these children hold such high vibrations and can resonate with those energies, they can also see into other planes of reality. Some can even speak different languages. I have only known a few children who did that in their sleep. I am sure we can all agree that we are not on the only plane of reality. Earth is not the only planet, so our children may share any number of different descriptions of "imaginary" friends. Just like us, there are many different souls or invisible friends out there who are curious and want to come and observe us. Some may even be terrifying to our children because of what we have described to them as being bad and scary. These other souls do not touch them and do not hurt them. They are simply curious, just like Grandma, who is coming to share moments with her grandchild.

It is important to know that there is no separation between their spiritual being and their earthly being. It is a part of their inner balance, the complete embodiment of who they are before they are grounded and mainstreamed into their humanness. Parents naturally become fearful and anxious because their everyday defenses cause much tension in their own energy field. Their own belief system breaks down their vibration, which triggers their vibration to stay in place and keeps them from seeing other planes of reality, so their child is seeing something they cannot and that is not acceptable to them. The need for higher vibration is essential to see spirits and/or other dimensional beings, and our chaos, anxiety, and mainstream belief systems lower our vibrations.

As I grew up and went from home to home, I never found other kids to connect with like myself and had to learn for myself how to survive with these abilities. It was hard, being so young without having others to guide me or calm me when I was overwhelmed or angry. No one taught me how to cope and how to control these emotions when those feelings got to be too much. Light bulbs would blow out, or things would fall from shelves. No one just understood. I had to discover things myself, finding out that it was a buildup of energy that caused those actions. Then I learned how to balance and control my emotions. I needed to learn how to break up the energy that built up in me from other people's energies, that would collect in me like I was a magnet. When someone is energy sensitive, they feel and collect others' thoughts and emotions until they learn how to block it. I learned early that when I was moving around, it helped release and clear the energy, and it made me feel better. Moving around constantly helps prevent the energy buildup that makes the sensitives feel uncomfortable. Then I had to learn what emotions were mine and what were someone else's, and that would help keep me in balance. Many of these lessons, I did not learn until I was an adult. I needed to understand how I could be here and also be with my spirit/soul friends, guides, family, whatever I needed at the time. The law of attraction and free will explains that, but no one in my life knew about that. I was my teacher.

When I became an adult with children and grandchildren of my own, I started to discover more children like me. This changed my life. I discovered I had a connection to young and old people who were like me. Some of these people had no idea of who they were because their human upbringing had clouded over who they really were. The children were loud and clear, and I could pick them out. They were the loudest, the most obnoxious, the children they labeled as ADD/ADHD or autistic or who had behavioral issues and could just not sit still. Some were even whimsical at that. I understood them. I saw them. I saw them when they were feeling happy and soaring around like an eagle does when it catches the wind current. They would recognize me as one of them as I passed them by. I saw the fear and frustration in their parents and the pain in their eyes and energy when they were at their wit's end, trying to figure out what was next for their child. Their one and only go-to answer was mental health and medication. I hated those words, *mental health*, and the treatment, *medication*. This resolution hurt me. I could hear and see these children, and I needed to find a way to help them. It became my passion, my mission in life, to help these children so they would not get medicated or institutionalized because no medical test explains them or what is happening. Maybe they did not need to be managed or medicated. Maybe they just needed to be understood. Maybe, just maybe, there was a natural solution to this, and nobody was seeing it or willing to look outside the medical mainstream. Could their environment, diet, or any other natural resource (or all of it) be triggering any of this?

These children started out in life remembering their past lives and having a sense of knowing. They were sensitive to energy and sound, and because of human grounding, these signs were ignored or unrealized, but still, underneath the clouded cover was a child like me. Now, in today's culture and with these children awakening us to who we are, we are starting to move toward the spiritual rather than the organized belief systems. I was introduced to these children, and I was excited beyond belief. I had no idea how this would all align in my life. I did not even know that this was going to be a part of my life's work. Finding who I was had given me the ability to help these children find a whole new world within themselves and teach them how to be themselves and to accept who they are. I did not want to change them. I wanted to show them how to be who they are, to live in this world, and show them that they are more normal than the people who call themselves normal. After all, we are all born this way. To do so, I had to educate their parents, showing them that their children are not part of a statistic or part of a doctor's diagnosis. This is extremely hard today.

I was about to put it all out there, expose who I am to people whom I have known for most of my life, and enter a realm that would alter my path, remembering that my greatest teachers were the ones who had challenged me the most—"the normal ones." I kept track of similarities between me and the children who came to me, discovering that the flux of kids coming into this realm now will indelibly alter our future. I was a part of a mystery, and now that mystery had multiplied in nature. My perception of life did not change. It was the worldview that slowly started to change. It was not just me anymore. There was now a huge flux of children who have been filling this world. They saw me, and I saw them.

As I started working with children and their past lives, I also met and worked with the parts of them that were causing issues. These kids tend to bounce all over the place and appear hyperactive and, many times, seem like they are not paying attention. Any type of discord in their families or around them would cause a meltdown. Sometimes it would result in what I called a short circuit. They would have seizures, and when they were tested, there was no general cause. This left the parent in complete, frantic fear, wondering what was wrong with their child and how they could help them. (Please, if your child does have a seizure, get medical treatment to be sure that it is not a medical reason first.) Each child whom I met thought that they were alone and different from all the other children in the world, and what their parents saw was a lifetime of medication and dysfunction. The result of this changed my life because it was now my mission to reach out and bring together many more children out there who were undiscovered and unrealized and who felt unconnected.

It has been my goal to bring to realization the fact that we are being awakened to an expansion of reality that past generations could not comprehend or even consider. The children who are being acknowledged are of another level, whose reality is more attuned to and who live between both worlds. These children will set a new norm for the ones who are labeled as "different," and I am blessed to be a part of it because I am not just a researcher and author. I am not just a regression therapist, medium, and meditation coach. I am one of them. As these children grow up, they grow up with the knowledge that they are "different," as society calls them, and always will be. It is not just some awkward stage; it is something we have known from birth. It has always been in the backs of our minds, how we fit in within our families. Sometimes we even feel like misfits and strangers to this world. As a kid, I related to the movie *ET* and felt his sadness and longing to "go home" as the world chased him so they could open him up and find out the mysteries ET held. We cannot be victims of who we are and the abilities we hold. These children know from the start that they are far more than physical beings and that their awareness functions at a much higher vibration. Going into big stores with many people and many sounds, energies, and moods, with too many things in their visual field, causes them to be overwhelmed and have much agitation. They need to move, run, jump around, and fidget to keep the flow of energy moving, or it has a physical effect on them. It makes them not feel well.

With all the gas industries and wells going up around the country, their noise, vibration, and energy cause unease and agitation in these children as well. I had first noticed this in myself when I was asked to come and cleanse someone's house because the energy and what they had described as spiritual happenings were making them ill and disrupting their animals. The previous tenant left for similar reasons. When I walked into this house, I felt the unease, and I did a strong cleansing of the house and got rid of all the residual energy. The house was calm, and people were happy. A few days later, it was back again. I went in the evening this time because I did not have the time during the day. As I pulled into the driveway, across the street from the house was a big lit-up gas well, and I felt it. It made me sick and dizzy. I could feel the vibration of the earth buzzing. That was it. That was what was causing all the discord. I reached in my bag, took out the stone I have learned to keep with me or preferably on me, and relaxed myself. Then I proceeded into the house to inform the tenants of the culprit that was causing all this disarray. I cleansed the house once again and told them that we needed a new course of action. I went home and pulled out my collection of crystals and stones—a few lodestones, tourmaline, obsidian, and a tiger's eye or two—and I went and placed them all around the inside of the house, all the rooms. I told the tenant that they needed to change them out and cleanse them once a week to rid the crystals of the energy they were absorbing as they were grounding the energy of the house. There was peace and calm after that. These hidden energies cause much havoc in the extremely sensitive, and with so much technology and the world changing to a world of such high-energy machines, our children are being affected. It does to me, and it does to our animals as well. We cannot stop the world from evolving and advancing in technology, so we need to find ways to protect the children and the highly sensitive.

One of the first things I do is talk to the parents and teach them how to raise these children and how to understand them. Yelling and harsh discipline do more harm than good and only create more chaos. Not believing them and telling them that what they know about when they were big or what they see is not real will cause more confusion. Certain foods and snacks that we give these children as well need to be looked at and changed. I find today that it is very vital that we give support to our children to help them understand and teach them how to be who they are. Just in the writing of this book, in a short period, five children have found their way to me with the same experiences of hearing voices and feeling emotional overload that leads them to destructive, dangerous actions such as cutting themselves or purposely hurting themselves. This is a form of sensory overload. Their energy fields absorb the input of their surroundings and those in it, and they do it more quickly than their minds can process. They cannot distinguish between what is theirs or someone else's. They can pick up peoples' thoughts and relate them to the voices in their own head. This is, again, not a mental disorder or a medical issue; it is sensory sensitivity. They need a creative outlet and a safe place. I practice the safe circle, where all judgment, anger, and worry is left outside the circle and all are free to talk, listen, and form an understanding of one another, no disagreements allowed. Whatever is said in that circle can never be judged.

When the child starts adolescence, all their hormone levels rise and fall in a fluctuating manner. Many changes, internally and externally, are happening. Emotions and feelings are added to this flux. Now add all these incoming stimuli with the fear of feeling different and being judged. They are not taught how to cope. We need to teach them this from the start of life, challenge them, and remind them about who they are. They are born to bodies that have open minds and logical and creative sides. We need to nurture both sides of their brains by stimulating them and exercising them with music and creative and critical thinking. I have always used music therapy to drown out the noises, but it is not your classic rap or everyday music. It is soft, meditative music that opens the creative brain and soothes the soul. It helps me focus because sometimes the silence is too loud.

We can start to help these children by accepting them, listening to them, and realizing that not all perceived learning disabilities or behavioral issues and medical or behavioral, they are just overly sensitive kids trying to find their way, trying to reach us and teach us. What if there is nothing wrong with them and we are just labeling them and throwing them to the wolves because of our own ignorance, our own fear of what is normal? The children I work with are highly intelligent and show it if they are allowed to expand outside their box and expectations that we force upon them. They teach us how to expand and evolve as well.

> What if in all our well-meaning efforts, we are tearing down the confidence and long-term productivity of the very children we mean to help? (Meg Blackburn Losey, PhD)

After working with these few children, I asked them if they liked who they are. If they could change who they are and be like all the other mainstreamed people in the world just to fit in, would they? They all told me one by one that yes, they now liked themselves and who they are, and no, they would not change that just to fit into the mainstreamed world. My dream is that these children whom I have worked with will reach out and help others who, for one reason or another, cannot find their calm, their normal. This is not just limited to the children of today; there are adults out there who are like this as well. We are *all* born this way. Our humanness and rules, societal expectations, and political correctness have buried our individual frequencies so deep down inside that it takes much work to bring them back and remember who we are. If we are determined not to listen or recognize what these children have to tell us through their past lives and their clear abilities, then our future is bleak. However, the positive is that the circle of life goes on, and as for the ones who uphold this mainstream life journey over these newly recognized children, these lessons will be loud and clear.

Everyone and everything is an expression
of the divine, including you.

— Cyndi Dale, *The Spiritual Power of Empathy*

EMPATHS

EMPATHS ARE PART of what I call a spectrum of the highly sensitives ones. If we were to look at the commonality between empaths and non-mainstreamed, sensitive children and adults, which we have talked about in this book, we can conclude that it is just another label describing the same basic ability. Empaths are described as extremely sensitive people who absorb both the stress and the good and bad emotions of the people around them. They feel everything to the extreme percent. They have what I describe as emotional short circuits from being overwhelmed by excessive stimulation and sensory overload. They do not have filters to block out stimulation. In other words, they are not human grounded and mainstreamed.

Today this seems to be the household superpower. Everyone is an empath. Is this true? My short, quick answer to that is we were born that way. So you would think my answer would be yes, but definitively, this is not a yes-or-no question because although we were all born highly sensitive, many of us were human grounded and mainstreamed into this life and have therefore buried deep and shorted out all our sensitivity, covered it up with what is called our "thick skin." We forgot who we are and what we are capable of. To put it bluntly, an empath has no walls, barriers, or shields like other people do. We are the "super responders." We are not big partygoers or those who gravitate to crowds because there is an overlap of our energy with others'. The sensation is intense and will make us feel anxious and tired at the same time because as the energy fields overlap, they drain us of our energy, giving us fatigue. Many times, I relate this feeling to Superman and kryptonite. They are emotional sponges, and they do not know how to release these emotions, so it all gets internalized—the feelings, the pain, all of it. The result of this can often give empaths this feeling of wanting to escape. Tones in people's voices affect me and can be triggers to responses, like how someone would react if they heard someone else scraping their nails on a chalkboard, and I was always known to act first before thinking.

Not much can be kept from me, including the truth, because I can always hear what people do not say; all they have to do is think it. This made Christmas fun. I always knew. I just had to ask, "What did you get me?" and the thought would come to their mind as they said, "It is a surprise!" I would smile, but I knew. Hearing what people do not say has its own challenges because I always knew when they were lying or when they were not telling me their true feelings. The flip side of that was I never had to second-guess. I personally hated areas like the mall at Christmas time. So much energy and so many emotions flying around—it made me anxious, tired, and moody. All these stimuli can agitate empaths because our threshold for sensory overload is extremely low. This is common for the highly sensitive and for empaths. While my friends were going to indoor concerts, I had to stay home. Weddings and crowds made me feel like I was suffocating. I was often labeled as being claustrophobic and odd because I did not like crowded places, and I did not want to be touched. The energy of their emotions and the sound of their thoughts sometimes blew me away and made me dizzy. In a crowd of people, it is much harder to pinpoint where the energy was coming from. I could, at times, feel it as an ache through my body, or if someone were to have physical pain, I could feel that as well, usually where their pain was located. For many years, I would have to constantly replace my vacuum; all the energy I absorbed would travel through me and short out my vacuum. Most empaths and highly sensitive children and adults discover who they are through their own higher self and intuition. They know themselves and have gone great lengths to control and hide who they are so as not to be viewed as different or weird. Throughout my life, I've discovered my intuition and learned to trust it to create my own tools and mindset to navigate through life, which helped me truly understand and claim my nature of who I am.

Infants and Children

Infants enter this world extremely sensitive, but some enter with more sensitivity than others. Those who are more sensitive have recently been incarnated here on Earth before and choose to bypass that waiting period between the birth and toddler stages and express themselves right away, showing early signs of these sensitivities. Some are just overlooked. Many are born to parents who are highly sensitive as well, although I have not seen any data on this as a trait being passed down. It is my knowing and belief that we were all born this way, fresh and new, with all-new senses, and attuned to all that surround us. It has been suggested that empaths may begin in utero, feeling the stress and joy of the mother. They emerge from the mother's womb extremely responsive to external stimuli. All the emotions that the mother goes through during pregnancy affect her unborn child, and it is known that the stress and anxiety of the mother creates the same in the fetus. They feel that vibration, like being in a tunnel and hearing and feeling all the vibrations of everything outside that tunnel. When the mother gets angry or anxiety sets in, her body vibrates and gets tense, and the baby feels that intense vibration. It has been said that the mother can pass on these anxieties to her child during pregnancy and birth. So would it be safe to say that the infant learns about anxiety and depression, among other human emotions, in utero, while the mother is pregnant? Could it be that simple?

We are humans, and as humans, although born with all our senses and highly sensitive abilities, we are not all alike. To say we are all the same would lead us to a conclusion that is contradictory to all life and a seemly senseless paradox. As humans, we are born as all humans are born—as one, a body with a soul. We are empathic. We are highly sensitive, with all renewed senses. It is within that oneness that we create our individuality and form our own reality, but we are conditioned by our human grounding, which is taught by our parents and those closest to us. As we come in and out of life, remembering the lives before and the lessons we are here to learn, we expand our vibrations and our souls, which will build on those abilities so as to evolve and create a better world.

These souls, our children, have been journeying home to us, telling us their stories, giving us messages, and teaching us about what life truly is and how our souls have been created for centuries, how we are supposed to evolve, and we put labels on them and discredit their journeys, calling them "special," "crazy," "imaginative," and "dysfunctional," along with many other labels. We define them as being different and put them in categories that separate them from the "normal" ones. I shake my head at the word *normal* because we live in a melting pot of differences in which being "different" is normal. So how is there a "normal" standard, and which difference sets that standard? Empaths and highly sensitive children understand the categories and labeling because they are, by nature, holographic thinkers and put everything in little compartments, but treating them differently makes them feel as if they do not belong, and that contributes to their low self-esteem. No matter what labels we put on these children—"empaths," "highly sensitive," "autistic"—to separate them from our "normal" standard, they are here to experience their "god" selves in human form, to contribute to the evolution of the soul, to educate us as humans about the true self, to expand human consciousness, and to reach our highest vibrations and universal connection. Even among the ones who write about these children and their abilities, they have also put labels on them and put them into categories. Their lists of identifying whether you are an empath, are sensitive, or have ADD, ADHD, or autism all have the same answers to the questions of what tie these people together as one. There are many similarities between the highly sensitive and the empathic:

- They have a hard time being around a lot of people. They leave crowded places feeling exhausted and anxious.
- They often retreat after exerting themselves. They need alone time to balance and recharge.
- They will gravitate to soft lighting versus harsh lighting. Fluorescent lights in stores are way too bright. They can hear the hum of these lights, and they are extremely loud.

- They do not like loud noises!
- They absorb and transmute the energies and emotions, the pains and stresses of other people around them. They find it extremely hard to know what their true feelings are and what emotions that they have absorbed and claimed as their own are someone else's. This can cause them to experience anxiety, depression, and panic attacks, with even some physical signs of increased heart rate and headaches. This comes from their reactive response to the absorbing and internalizing of emotions because they do not have the ability to distinguish others' feelings and emotions from their own feelings and emotions.
- They will often get agitated if you violate their space or touch them or their personal stuff without their permission for the simple reason that they can feel, hear, and sense all your emotions and thoughts with every touch.
- They are often told that they are too sensitive and need to grow a backbone.
- They have unexpected anxiety or unexplained energy, often centered in their chest, which comes on without any reason. This could feel like little flutters.
- They do not like confrontational episodes and do not like to argue, but on the flip side, they are usually right. That type of energy makes them feel physically ill. Any type of negativity hurts them, including lying.
- They are known to hold feelings in so they do not upset others and create a flow of negative energy.
- They attract people who are in desperate need of emotional support, and everyone finds them, even strangers, for that emotional support.
- They attract people with narcissistic personalities who think that they can appeal to and take advantage of their sensitive side.
- They are highly active and may seem to "bounce off the wall" or rock back and forth.
- They move stagnant energy to spread and disperse it.

- They attune to what literally everyone is feeling and their conditions, such as anger, severe anxiety, depression, eating disorders, sadness, loneliness—all emotions. This can all be manifested within them on a constant basis, and none of these feelings, conditions, and emotions originate within themselves; it is all other people.

Both empaths and the highly sensitive feel that their personal world is continually invaded by the energy and emotions of those around them. This can exhaust them and drain them of their energy, like a battery's life being drained in the sun. For example, I went to a friend's house to counsel them about something we were working with. They have two children who are highly sensitive and have, on occasion, had overloads, and they were labeled as being part of what doctors call the "spectrum." One of them at the time was at the age of puberty. When I had arrived and walked into this house for our meeting, I felt an immediate gush, like someone had just thrown an energy ball right at me. During that whole time, I could not sit still. I got all jumbled up with words, finding it hard to finish sentences, and could not find the words to express my thoughts. The energy was felt through me, so it tickled my throat and I needed water to calm the cough. When I left, I immediately took off my shoes, placed my bare feet on the earth and closed my eyes to push out all the energy I had just absorbed from that house. I was exhausted and had to rest to recharge. Normally, I have my crystals and protection tools on me, but for some reason, I had forgotten to put them back on after taking them off to be cleansed that day.

This leads me to another common aspect of being an empath or highly sensitive. Going outside and connecting with nature feels like an essential part of their lives. It is a need. Most empathic, highly sensitive children do not like shoes and are very nature oriented. It helps ground them. They feel free, and they can naturally disperse the energy buildup. They truly are not ones to be locked in the house all day. Many doctors have diagnosed them with ADHD/ADD/Asperger's/autism and medicated them because there is no other medical reason and they fall into the guidelines they have set for them. The number of medicated children is astonishing and should be alarming. Doctors are looking at the outer self and not the inner self.

The thinking process of an empath or highly sensitive person is not linear. They compartmentalize, which is said to be bad for most, but with empathic and highly sensitive children, it is essential because they absorb information constantly from having access to subtle information stored in the energy field of all types of life forms. They need to put it into compartments to utilize later on, or they would be in constant overload, like putting sixty-four gigabytes of files into a thirty-two-gigabyte hard drive, which does not work. They have an incredibly open personal energy field, giving them the ability to merge with any life force and absorb its energy. They often experience the ability to understand and hear the thoughts of others and can answer questions that someone else is thinking. This ability was the one that had outed me. They get told by others to get out of their heads because they know what the other person is thinking. Although to many, this ability may seem creepy, to empaths and the highly sensitive, it is a form of protection. They can always tell who is good or bad and if someone likes them or dislikes them, no matter what the other person says. Most empaths and highly sensitive people have a hard time with self-love and creating boundaries and often have no filter when they know something is right, when someone is telling them they are wrong, or when they are being touched or something of theirs is being touched without their permission. They let you know, sometimes loudly.

We empaths have many intuitive gifts, known as "clairs," that we are born with and that are tools for our senses, and that is what we are meant to use them for. Many of these abilities are within our inner selves.

Clairvoyance: The empath receives clear visions as well as extrasensory impressions and symbols within their inner sight by reaching into their vibrational frequency and visually perceiving the impression through their mind's eye.

Clairempathy: The empath receives clear emotions. This is a type of telepathy to sense and feel within one's self another life force or entity by tuning into the vibrations and feeling the tones of the aura that surround it. The other "clair" related to this one is the next one.

Clairsentience: The empath receives clear sensations or feelings throughout the whole body without physical stimuli, such as walking into a room and feeling the words and emotions of the people there or determining if people were there. They can also sense portals and other vibrational fields.

Clairalience: The empath experiences clear smelling, able to smell something not within their personal surroundings.

Clairaudience: The empath experiences clear hearing, able to hear sounds, words, mental tones, and vibrational tones from within this realm and outside of it.

Clairgustance: The empath experiences clear tasting without putting something in their mouth, tasting the "essence."

Clairtangency: The empath experiences clear touching, able to touch something and pick up information from it. Most with this ability will shy away from shaking hands or hugging because they can see and feel what you're hiding. Your pain hurts them.

Types of Empaths and Highly Sensitive People

As there are different "clairs" that describe the abilities of empaths and highly sensitive children, so are there many different skills that are adopted. Some are more pronounced than others. Most who realize their abilities and want to build them up surround themselves with only the energies that serve them. Through these skills, you can begin to understand how your child can evolve, and this will help you explore who your child is before the world begins to influence and mainstream them and before your child loses their center. Children, as they grow and they are mainstreamed into this judgmental world, will lose their centers and forget who they were born to be. Recognizing and understanding them helps them, from the beginning of life, feel centered and confident in who they are, and they will know how to fit in and won't feel scared or like they do not belong here. They will know through you that they are here to open our eyes and to change the world. They are here to bring us back to love and to remember our true selves and our true purpose. Some of these collective sensitivities will become stronger. Some children will evolve and grow with all their open senses and use them all while, others will just use the ones that serve them best. Then there are those who will ignore them, and it will affect them for life.

Here is a breakdown of different kinds of empaths:

Emotional Empaths: This is the prime kind. They absorb others' energy and emotions like a sponge.

Physical Empaths: They take on and feel the physical ailments of other people.

Intuitive Empaths: They are energetically sensitive, psychic, and telepathic by nature and can have precognitive gifts as well, such as intuitive dreaming, astral projection, and precognition.

Telepathic Empaths: They receive thoughts and impressions from others.

Mediums: They are able to communicate with those vibrating at a higher level or who have journeyed on. Many mediums can hear, feel, sense, and taste spirits. Children are born mediums, and many come here with messages from loved ones. My granddaughter has always seen and spoken with people who have journeyed on. She makes it a point every morning to say hello to the guy at the top of the stairs. She often puts her arms up for them to pick her up. If you watch your children and listen, they will tell you. My son and I are both empathic and sensitive. We were never mainstreamed, so we can experience this vibrational connection. We are fully aware of who my granddaughter is speaking and signing to.

Nature Empaths: They are sensitive to weather patterns and planetary movements, and they can pick up energy emitted by animals. The abilities I have with this kind of empathy are very weak. I can feel the ground move when at sea level, even get nauseous from it. I can feel the air when a storm is on the way, hear the whispers of the wind, and connect with my herbs and plants—and yes, I am a tree hugger. I see the air around me. I can understand my own personal feline, and we have many conversations. That is the extent of my ability as an earth empath or sensitive person, but I know people who can do far more than that, and they are nature empaths. My granddaughter can also be seen talking to the flowers and the trees and what I call faerie energies in the herb garden.

Her mind is lost,
Lost at sea.
She lost herself
And who she'd be.
She'll get better.
Just watch; she'll show
How brave she is,
And watch her grow.
She's beautiful inside,
Despite all the pain.
That little girl is okay,
And she's actually sane.

— Lizzy Travis

MISCONCEPTIONS OF HIGHLY SENSITIVE AND EMPATHIC CHILDREN

M ANY OF THE things I talk about in this book have been misunderstood, and empaths and the highly sensitive are at the top of that list. There is a misconception among people that being an empath or a highly sensitive person is just another fad or a momentary feeling that they experience, and as they say, "this too shall pass." This is not in any way true. They are not defined by their feelings, and it is not just a character trait. This ability is not something that we turn on inside ourselves when someone we love or care about is going through hard times. It is not a state of mind or an emotional state. There is no on-and-off switch. Empaths and highly sensitive people must learn how to control it and still live their daily lives hoping not to be judged or ridiculed by people who just have no idea or understanding. This is something that they live with 24-7. There is no gimmick or parlor trick. They are not evil. There is no magic whatsoever. They have a highly sensitive nervous system that requires extra-vigilant self-care. They are over-giving and put themselves last. They are the children who come home from school crying because their best friend got a boo-boo on his knee and it hurt. They are the ones who will give the little girl who has no lunch their favorite sandwich.

Empaths put value on what is essential and the things that this world has so little of—peace, harmony, calmness, and freedom from stress—and the biggest, most important value is love. These are the children who have unexplained tantrums, who are chronically sick with the cold, the flu, asthma, and stomach upsets, usually when they are around a group of chaotic and emotionally charged people. Their mental state affects their physical state through illness. Strong smells, noises, tastes, and textures cause a bad reaction among highly sensitive children. They do not deal well with other people and/or children. They act out more when other people are stressed or angry. Their moods or behavior will undergo extreme shifts. They will have a hard time focusing on a thought or a project. Sometimes they may just shut down because they cannot handle it with all that is going on and can be found in a corner, away from others. They can also find their solace in nature or around animals.

I knew a little boy from the time he was born. He is not mainstreamed and has all the abilities he was born with, and from an early age, we saw it. Many people thought he was just poorly disciplined, and keeping a babysitter was so hard for his single mom. He was always active. It seemed like he was having the most joyous time. His nickname from me was Mr. Giggles because he was having the time of his life, "bouncing off the walls," as some people would call it. He was always giggling, and all he wanted was for you to laugh, giggle, and play too. As he got older, we noticed that he did not like being touched or restrained in any way, which made that even harder for his single mom. Putting him in car seats and even holding his hand at the store was next to impossible. He had a routine; if that routine was changed, there was an issue with this little guy.

With an active child, you're always behind in time. You are always getting frustrated because they are running around and because Mommy must be somewhere at a certain time, so yes, moms get frustrated. That frustration causes energy. That energy, to this little guy, was negative, and it hurt. He could feel her frustration in her energy and her touch, and he reacted to it. They figured this out and went through many different challenges, adjustments, routines—and yes, babysitters. Years down the road, when he was on the onset of puberty, things started to change again. We are right in the middle of a pandemic, and routines change; emotions are flying and at their peak. All this was building up in this little guy. He started to bounce off the walls again. Some of these things drew concern. Mom had to establish a new routine to maintain peace and create a safe space for him to release this energy. One extremely helpful item was a weighed blanket for when he started bouncing. They got through that, and the doors opened for us to be able to get out of our home and be around small groups of people. Now this little guy could run and move, and being outside, feet on the ground, helped him cleanse and release that energy. As he was outside, he discovered that down the road, there was a wedding going on, so off he went. Mom had no idea where he went. Panic set in. She ran around the neighborhood, calling his name in sheer fright of what might have happened to her son. Now remember—he is not a toddler, so being outside without supervision is okay.

Soon, she heard, "I am here, Mom," and sure enough, he was.

He had crashed the wedding. Everyone at the wedding thought he was the cutest thing, and they were laughing and so happy to have him as their guest. There was a sense of relief from knowing he was okay. There was still the question as to why he just up and did that. The answer was simple in my eyes. I told his mom that at a wedding, everybody is happy. All the energy was full of love and happiness, and that went right along with Mr. Giggles. It made him feel happy, and he needed that.

When a baby is in the womb, they say that stress, anger, and negative feelings hurt the baby, so it is essential not to cause the unborn trauma with the mother's anxiety and stress. We say, "Relax. Calm down." So if this is a true scientific and medical diagnosis, then why are we not seeing it when our children are born? Do we think that they suddenly do not feel energy? How can we put labels like "evil" and "mentally ill" or "devilish" on them when all they seek is happiness and love? All they want to do is belong. Is that not human nature—to desire belonging? At the human level, they need validation and to realize that they are understood and not crazy or alone. They need not to be medicated but to be taught self-care.

In this fast-paced world, where single parents are raising their families and the cost of living is high, the breakdown of family structure and routine is different from what it was, say, ten years ago. Kids are becoming more independent at a young age; family interactions are falling to the side. Values are not being taught, and family culture is not being recognized, so children are not being mainstreamed, and that is okay if you recognize it and nurture it. Children today hold on to the abilities they were born with and are forming new ways of being. They are holding onto their sensitive ways. That is why there are more kids being medicated. Most of the parents of these kids were born and raised in families with strict cultures and beliefs that hid and buried the abilities we as souls being born into humanness were born with. This is not new. We have all been born sensitive and empathic, but when we told our stories about when we were big or when we heard voices from beyond, we were automatically told it was wrong—"Do not talk crazy like that" and so on. The town minister would come and counsel and try to banish that evil out of us. Soon, we were mainstreamed. Some families were structured with strict upbringings, heritages, and cultures that you did not dare venture from. There was no room to be anything less or more than what our parents wanted us to be. We were flooded with an abundance of images, stereotypes, ideals, cultures, religious beliefs, and values. They set the standard of what is acceptable and taught what is right and wrong by their standards. They conditioned their children with labels and stereotypes. "Boys are this way, and girls are that way. Boys do not cry, and girls are overly dramatic."

The act of sensitivity has a stigma attached to it that does not include the core emotional and psychological levels of who they are. They get taught to hide their emotions and pretend to be the same as others so they can be accepted and blend in. That type of social conditioning can affect them and shape their personalities and insecurities. Parents and loved ones—out of frustration, tiredness, and anger—imprint their emotions onto their sensitive children by lashing out with anger, maybe out of frustration, calling them stupid, useless, idiots, or plain bad. These children feel these emotions, internalize them as truth, and believe what their loved ones have told them. After a while, they learn to completely ignore their own feelings and their self-esteem, and their vibration lowers. Negative core beliefs form.

They are not magnets to negative energy. They get congested with other people's dumping of emotional energy. It is the emotional outer climate that makes them congested. They are definitely not fragile. After all, they are carrying a world of emotions, pain, and karma from others and themselves. They know what you are thinking and how you feel about them. They carry and identify with others' feelings, stress, and anxiety and take them on as their own. After all that, they are still standing, and this happens on a constant basis. This is not a weak, fragile person. They are not self- absorbed; it is you they care about, more than themselves.

All these negative energies, if not noticed and not nurtured, can create toxins for an empathic or sensitive child, anger being the most toxic and destructive. Anger is a powerful energy that is absorbed and creates a more potent energy within a sensitive and empathic child, partly because they take it on as their own emotion. They need understanding and to be taught to cope and care for themselves. What they are not is evil; they are normal and born this way. They do not need to be put in hospitals. They need to be recognized and understood by parents and the ones who take care of them and, most of all, the medical field. We are medicating our children and putting labels on them. This may not seem like a big study, but in one week in my small town, I asked parents about their children and how they were coping, and fifteen to twenty kids were diagnosed with and medicated for ADD, ADHD, autism, Asperger's, and other mental illnesses. Fifteen out of twenty? *Seriously?* Is there something in our water, or are we really missing something? Five-year-olds in the psychiatric wards in hospitals? Could it be that these kids, while they are completely vulnerable to their surroundings, are multi-sensitive with a refined ability to connect with the soul essence of everything around them? Like I mentioned before, given our fast-paced world, our demand for both parents to work to maintain their lifestyles, and the high rate of single parents, the strict family structure and religious authority have fallen to the wayside. Therefore, our children are holding on to what they were born with. This, for some, can be perceived as a curse, but in reality, it is a blessing. It is what we seek all our lives.

As we get older, we have a desire to reunite with the universe or what some call God to experience what we felt at birth—a oneness and an atonement with the universe, God, the source, whichever name you call it. We want to know the senses of the soul—intuition, peace, foresight, trust, and empathy. We want the full experience of our human senses that give us such joy and peace—touch, smell, taste, sight, and hearing. This is who we are. This is who we were born to be. We are now experiencing this flux of children whom we do not understand, and our instincts that were imprinted in us from our upbringing tell us that there is something wrong, that our children are sick. Doctors have no real rhyme or reason, no blood tests or CT scans, nothing to show illness. Their diagnosis comes from the words, actions, and behavior of the child. They put labels on and medicate them. What they do not see or understand is that their humanness has provided them with physical episodes in life that touch on their sensitivities and abilities and that these abilities come from the soul, not the body's brain, and left unrecognized, they cause a sensitive child to go into overdrive, with no tools to use to escape. Medicine and labels do not fix them. Teaching them self-care does. We need to realize that by only looking at the outer parts of humans, we are harming the inner parts of our humanness. We need to accept that we are minds, bodies, and souls and that we have to connect them to create our oneness. If this does not resonate with you, find something that will. It is imperative to make time alone for you and your child to decompress and reconnect. Without this time, their nervous system will fry easily, and that is when the out-of-control, disruptive behavior and meltdowns will happen. If this does happen, I suggest not to scream or show anger but use a calm voice, and a weighted blanket is highly recommended. Get them to focus on your eyes and practice slow breathing with them. When they have calmed down, acknowledge the emotion, talking about how they feel and what is making them feel this way. Try and keep eye contact. Your child may sporadically look away, but you must stay focused and bring him/her back to your eyes. Stop for a few minutes and take some relaxing breaths. Keep your voice calm. Remember that whatever energy you are transmitting will influence your child, so be mindful of your own energy. When you are stressed, tired, and cranky, your mindset will follow, and you will focus on the negative. You need to acknowledge this, breathe, and focus on happy thoughts. If possible, take a "me" break. I dance it out. It changes the atmosphere. It brings in the most powerful of all energies, laughter, and that will change to love. You can also take your child to a sacred spot where you can use your senses to hear the earthly sounds, look at wildlife if you are in a spot to do so, smell the air. Just take it all in. Put your feet in running water and feel the stress trickle out the bottom of your feet and float away. Do not let your crankiness linger because it is only downhill from there.

Create in your home a peaceful, calming environment. If your whole house cannot be done that way, make one room. I did an experiment in my house. I have a corner in my living room set up for my writing so that I can still write if I need to reach deadlines and manage my crystal meditation shop when the grandbabies are over. I play soft instrumental meditation music, turned down low. My playlist comes from Spotify. I play it all the time, even at night, when all are sleeping. It is extremely low and light music. Some music is elemental, like waterfalls and rain. I diffuse light scents like lavender, and the lighting, when people are up and about, is low—not dark, just low. I did this for a month, and it changed the energy from crazy and chaotic to calm, peaceful, and happy. When people came over, after they left, I smudged the house to maintain the peaceful atmosphere. This helped me become able to write and meet deadlines. An empathic, sensitive child or adult has a hard time completing tasks that require their thought if they are stressed. It is hard enough when the work I do requires technology because that too can cause energy overload. Even if I am on a deadline, I take breaks and decompress, or I will be wasting time spinning in my chair, getting nothing or very little done. All this applies to children as well. The only benefit that an adult has over a child is understanding. If you are fifty and do not understand what is happening and who you are, then you are at the same level as a child empath.

There's something about her
That nobody knows.
She shines on the outside,
But inside, the darkness grows.

— Lizzy Travis

HIGHLY SENSITIVE EMPATHIC
TEENS AND PUBERTY

Emily Denzel
2021

BEING A TEENAGER and going through the body, mind, and soul changes that come with growing up is a major rite of passage. There are so many changes, and highly sensitive or empathic teens' abilities are extremely amplified. Their hormones are flooding through their bodies as nature finds a way of transforming the child into an adult—body, mind, and soul. Being an empath is not new, but they have been mainstreamed and masked by the conditioning of their parents and family and what our culture has taught them. They may feel bombarded, murky, sick, or imbalanced, especially at this time of change.

At puberty, a sensitive/empathic child's energy expands, and hormones rage. Conflicting feelings that were suppressed emerge, and memories of their past lives can emerge again. This time, "Mommy, when I was big" becomes scary. They were judged and told when they were young children that this was wrong, so these memories now seem like familiar nightmares. This is a time where everything we were imprinted with and the memories of the past collide. At a young age, a child begins to form their dark side (shadow side), where all the mainstreaming teaches them to separate our world into good/right and bad/wrong. All our beliefs, ideals, superstitions, and moral code are created. What we are taught that is bad/wrong gets buried in our dark side, where all is hidden and suppressed. The dark side remains within our unconscious mind, and with the onset of puberty, it emerges through our subconscious. When this emerges, it is an immensely powerful and intense feeling. Hidden thoughts come to the surface and get questioned. All the abilities that they had at birth that were suppressed come out with a vengeance, creating a tailspin of emotions. With this, they become overwhelmed.

As teenagers, they may feel the intense emotions of love for a romantic partner for the first time or jealousy and even, if taught, hate. They do not know what to do with these extreme emotions because they have never felt them, so they were never taught. They are in between the stages of being a child and being a teen. Conflicts and challenges occur between teens and adults. They separate themselves from their parents to establish a functional independence, becoming one with who they are while trying to figure out who that is among all the mainstreaming that was taught to them throughout life. They feel that no one hears them and that they are highly misunderstood. They know they are different. They feel that they are. All the thoughts and emotions that were locked away in their dark side are at the forefront of their minds, and no one listens. No one tells them it is natural for this to happen. These thoughts and feelings are real and natural. They change how they look and are more conscious of their outer selves, some even changing their whole outer selves, trying to create unique identities while trying to fit in. Many teens are unable to understand or communicate their distressed, confused emotions. As unrecognized, highly sensitive, empathic teens, they are at a higher risk of acting out or falling into depression. Feeling unheard, misunderstood, and alone, they reach a desperate point of self-destruction.

Parents need to recognize this and communicate their recognition to their child, show them their approval of their new identity, place themselves in their teenagers' place, say thing like "If I were in your situation, I would feel hurt and angry also" and "I remember when I was your age and I did that or felt that way." Explain how you felt and how the situation worked out, and they too can make it through. They are at that age of rebellion. Before highly sensitive children hit puberty, many of them are not taught to set boundaries. There has been such a breakdown in raising and teaching children these days when it comes to common, basic lessons in life. Shoot, most do not even have a filter. What a combination that can be!

Our boundaries for empaths and highly sensitive people are like layers of skin that cover and protect our physical bodies. Setting our boundaries preserves and supports our emotional and mental health. These boundaries are like a protective energy that helps keep us strong and maintain a well-balanced sense of self. For empaths and the highly sensitive, this is extremely essential. This mindset requires you to be mindful and aware of the way you perceive your energetic space. Having these boundaries will help us distinguish between our own emotions and thoughts and those of others. For a teen who is going through this major flux and the changes in their lives, not having boundaries can be extremely chaotic and dangerous. It stands a chance of impacting the next phase of their life and their adulthood. It can create an immense amount of psychological issues and much anxiety that will create more overload and breakdowns. It can be the catalyst between life and death in an unbalanced teen. In this time in a teen's life, it is imperative to approach it slowly and gently, with love and sincerity, an open mind, and an open soul.

My insides are dying.
My outsides are broken.
Everyone knew it,
But nobody spoke.

— Lizzy Travis

SELF-CARE AND MANAGEMENT

I T IS ESSENTIAL that we first recognize who we are and who our children are. We are souls first. As infants, we feel the oneness and atonement of who we are. This is not just an empathic, sensitive experience. It is who we are before the world changes us. We try so hard to hold onto this, but cultures and other mainstream ideas and beliefs mask us. This is who we are and born to be, whether we want to be or not.

What we have failed to do as parents is teach the essentials, like boundaries, knowing one's identity, acceptance, coping skills, and decompressing. These should be core essentials in raising children. When working with parents, one of the first things I tell them—and I express it as one of the most essential things they need to do—is to let go of their ego and their mainstream thought patterns, come out from behind their masks, and know themselves. It is important for the parent to recognize the senses of the soul so they can help their children. Get rid of the fear that was imprinted in you as part of your upbringing. Let go of melodramatics and find their center. I hear all the time, "I do not have time for this" and "This is too much change." Without change, without the understanding and acceptance of who our highly sensitive children are or who we are meant to be, without showing them compassion, they remain in a painful, chaotic state of unpredictable emotions. Make an appointment, an hour two days a week to start. Make it a priority. Sensitive/empathic children and adults need to decompress and center their focus and attention because of the high levels of stimulus that surround them. Take yourself and your children out of the electronic world. Turn off the phones and tablets. Dim the lights because the highly sensitive are affected by bright lights. Play some soft meditation music and breathe. One technique I enjoy that works well with me as an empath is this. I sit and close my eyes, with my meditation music playing, breathe out all my stress, and slowly start to move, with the soft music dispersing the energy. I can feel the tingles in my body as I move the energy, like a slow dance. I keep breathing in and out, pushing all the energy that is building up within me out. Then I take my clear quartz, cacoxenite (with Super 7), smoky quartz, and snowflake obsidian or whatever speaks to me that day, but these four are my go-to. The clear and smoky quartz help with my grounding and releasing all the built-up energies. Snowflake obsidian purifies and clears my body, heart, mind, and spirit of toxins created through the negative energies and grounding. I use cacoxenite for reprogramming to renew my body, clearing my third eye and all the chakras and balancing them, expanding my consciousness, creating a balance within my soul. I also make sure that after people who have come to visit leave, I smudge the areas, dispersing all their energies. I do leave the bedroom doors closed, not because they might be messy but to keep other peoples' energies from entering my somber place. I also have some sacred items that I keep in my room that I do not want touched, such as crystals, cards, and divination tools. Some people like to display these things in the main rooms of their homes. I do not so as not to pick up the energies that I do not want in these items. I do, on the other hand, have items that are working with the energies of the house, which I do have displayed and cleansed regularly.

Use crystals and stones to help balance your children. Use Himalayan sea salt lamps to emit radiation and prevent an overexposure to electromagnetic energy. These emit a large sum of negatively charged ions into the air. I have one in each room. Stones and crystals, I use regularly, such as tiger's eye, black obsidian, tourmaline, hematite, and amethyst. I not only have them around my home but also wear them and carry them in my pocket. Some people believe that certain stones are self-cleansing, but I am not of that thought. I have seen crystals, such as clear quartz, that many say is self-cleansing turn cloudy, even dark, and shatter while the person is wearing it. So I do recommend cleansing your crystals, even the ones you wear.

Teach your empathic children that everything is not their responsibility. They are young, so they do not understand that what they are perceiving from others—their needs, motivations, actions, and choices—are not their responsibility because they feel it themselves from others. They will do everything they can to make them happy and please the people around them. They need to know that it is nice to help them, but these are not their emotions to own. The child's own needs need to come first. Teach them what their own emotions feel like so they can identify them. Encourage them to tell you when they are overwhelmed, tired, or angry, even happy or sad. Express to them that they need to help themselves first.

Give them a healthy safe space. Do not be a helicopter parent. Let them go to this place when they feel overwhelmed. If your child does not like being around certain people, give them the permission to tell you and allow them to not be around those people. Do not force them into a social situation with extracurricular and social commitments. Allow them to make their own choices as to which social commitment they want to be a part of. If your child says that they do not want to be around Aunt Lisa and Uncle Frank today, then ask them why and listen to what they say. Let them be in their room (supervised if they are not old enough to be alone) or with another supervising adult. This does not always mean that Aunt Lisa and Uncle Frank are bad people. It is just that their energy is uncomfortable for your child that day. Maybe they had a bad day or a fight. Maybe they are upset or anxious about something or even sick and that energy is making your child feel uncomfortable. I do caution though that your child will feel dangerous people, and it is important to listen to them and follow through in identifying what it is that makes your child feel this way. By all means, respect your child's wishes.

Communicate with your child, especially when something is wrong. As I have repeated over and over, your child is highly perceptive of everything going on around them. They know when you are off or feel troubled, and they feel it. Tell your child when something is off or has gone out of sync. You do not have to share the details. Just tell them, "I am anxious today" or "Daddy had a hard day and is cranky." That way, your child knows it is not them and that they did nothing to hurt you because whether or not you want them to know, they do, and they feel it. You must make it your goal to stay as centered as possible, and if you're off, say, "Mommy is off today. She needs her safe place." Some ideas of other things you can do are meditation, yoga, and mindfulness. Show your child that Mommy practices these things and allow them to do it with you. It creates a pattern and bonding as well as teaches them to identify and disperse their built-up energy. You are also teaching them that what they are feeling is not wrong.

Being self-aware will help your child immensely and create an environment your child can thrive in. Teach them daily affirmations. Make some index cards with affirmations on them and have your child draw one each day, face the mirror, and repeat the affirmation, things such as "I am only responsible for my feelings," "My life is full of love for life and other people," and "I love the person I am." Make sure that your affirmations are uplifting and set a positive tone. Stay calm, happy, and loving and shake out any negative energy or thoughts that might be lingering. Practice deep breathing, and often, during your day, take a moment to take one conscious deep breath to release tension and recharge. Do not be afraid to say, "I need alone time" and take it. Say what you mean and follow through.

Educate the people who are around your child and set up a plan with his or her teachers. Explain that your child tends to experience sensory overload. Warning: be prepared for feedback and different responses. Remember—this is your child. These are your child's needs and your decisions, whether they believe you or agree or not. Set up a safety plan with their teachers. Creating a Zen space would be beneficial to all children and could really be beneficial in the education system. Do not allow the bullying, judging, or criticizing of your child. Show your child that you support them. They need to feel safe. Explain to them that the bully is the one with the issues. The bully has emotional problems, not them. Send zero tolerance toward bullies. Learn to deal with your own frustrations and teach them to deal with their own, or they will grow to be demanding and self-centered. I noticed that when I came home from work all frustrated and wound up, my children would become whiny and act out, and that would then send a chain reaction of chaos throughout the house and create stress for all. With this observation, I made some beneficial changes to my drive home from work. I would put soft, upbeat, happy music on my car stereo, take some deep breaths, and release all the frustration until the next workday. This is called letting go and leaving your work at work. Doing this changed the whole energy and outcome of the evening. I was in a more relaxed mood, and my energy was calmer and more loving. The same thing happened for my children.

Intervene before tantrums flare up.

Set reasonable and clear boundaries and enforce them, remembering that it is okay to say no. Give them choices, and when you need to find a solution but want them to make the choice, say something like this: "I know you want to do this, but you can only do it if you do this first." This will show them that there are boundaries and that they can get what they want, but it is give and take. You need to follow through. Teach coping skills. Do not say things like "Man up," "Only babies cry," or "You're too sensitive, too soft, unmanly, less of a woman," or less of anything. These statements degrade and lessen the self-esteem of the sensitive person, in the end damaging the sensitive person.

Create your Zen space at your home for your child with things such as a dark space, light music, a weighted blanket, noise-canceling headphones, indoor plants, diffusers, salt lamps, and crystals. This will soothe their nervous system. Teach them how to work with their gifts. Teach them how to turn down stress by dimming the lights and turning on calming and soothing music or nature sounds, such as rain and waterfalls. Take a deep breath, exhaling stress. Slow down your vibration. Set bedtimes that allow at least eight hours of solid sleep and turn off all electronics two hours before bed.

Teach relaxation techniques, such as the following:

Younger Children

- Breathing exercises
- Yoga
- Visualization
- Blowing bubbles
- Banging drums

- Creative dance
- Meditation
- Crystal therapy
- Storytelling
- Scarf dancing (my one-year-old granddaughter loves this)
- Qigong

Older Children (Teens)

- All of the above
- Breathing
- Meditation
- Creative art
- Color therapy
- Creative dance
- Qigong

Give them plenty of outside nature time for grounding, releasing, and recharging.

Look at your child's diet. Food carries energy. Some have bad energy, while others have good energy, all of which can affect your mood as well as your body–mind–soul connection.

Bad-Energy Foods

- Processed food
- Saturated fats
- Sugar and artificial sweeteners
- Preservatives and salt
- GMOs (genetically modified organisms)
- Gluten
- Dyes

Good-Energy Foods

- Vegetables
- Whole grains
- Legumes
- Nuts
- Fruits

Pay attention to your body. Certain fruits will work against some sensitive people. Every person is different. Limit meats and animal products.

Reduce exposure to stimuli such as violent video games or television shows—energy vampires. If energy vampires cannot be avoided because you are in a store or other places that you cannot leave at that moment, teach your child techniques on how to stay grounded and get through it while the emotions pass through. These emotions, when absorbed, can be scary and confusing for a child. They need to feel accepted and loved exactly as they are. The lower their self-esteem and self-love, the more toxic the energy they can take in, and as a result of this, they can have periods of feeling lost and disconnected from their higher self, the divine or the source.

Declutter your house. When there is a lot of clutter scattered around, it becomes too busy for your sensitive child. Everything competes with their attention, making it harder for them to focus. When this happens to me, my son calls me a squirrel. I am focused on one thing, and just like that, something else gets my attention, and I am there. Then something else happens, and I am there, and so on. I get like that when cleaning as well, especially when it is after an event and there is so much to clean. It takes a lot to focus on one thing at a time. It is too much. I exhaust myself. When my highly sensitive grandkids come over, I will have all the toys nicely in the toy box. They start off with one toy, but then another toy they see gets their attention and then another. They cannot play with them all together, so they play with them separately, bouncing from one toy to the next. When lunchtime comes and I have anything on the table where they sit, they get anxious, and they have to move everything, even if it is on the other side of the table, not even close to any of them, because they say they have to give their food the attention. If there is stuff there, they will have to touch it. I have remedied all those issues by only taking out a few of their favorite toys and leaving the toy box in another room. When it comes time for lunch, everything is in its place.

Encourage them to write on a journal without having to wear a proverbial mask. If they've had a bad day, have them write what they feel—no sugarcoating. Let them draw pictures about how they feel. This exercise will help them release what they feel. This will help them tune into their feelings, and if they need to cry, let them. Teach them to be more objective and open to what they are feeling. Break it down and have them answer questions to enhance the healing journey and build critical thinking. This will teach them how to separate their feelings from someone else's. They need to know that honesty is required. These are the questions that they need to ask themselves every time they have an issue or that you, as a parent, can ask them to help them through what they are feeling. Ask pointed questions to clarify concepts and help them think it through and analyze the irrational thought:

- What made you feel this way?
- Did you choose to feel this emotion?
- What is the emotion you are feeling?
- What is the reason for this emotion?
- Do you know if this reason is 100 percent true?
- Why or how do you know this?
- What is the evidence for this emotion?
- What is the evidence against this emotion?
- Is this your feeling or someone else's?

This will help them think it through. Then ask them how they feel now. This will help balance their heart with their head. Your part as a parent is to validate them and support them, telling them that their sensitivity is a valuable gift, that their gifts are their own superpowers. Explain to them that many will not understand them, and that is okay.

The ones who want to understand you will, and others will not, and that is okay. It is normal to feel different. We are all different. That is what makes us all special in our own way. Tell them their abilities and differences are what make them perfect in every way because along with these superpowers, they have the power of kindness, loving hearts and souls, and they are intelligent and thoughtful. Being all this, sometimes they will feel tired and sad around others, and that too is okay. Be mindful of how you express your emotions to and around your children. Acting out of frustration will leave then upset and confused.

Most of all, tell them they are not ever broken.

TRISH AVERY

What if I never existed
And this was all a dream?
What if I never existed,
More like a nightmare?
What if I never existed,
Staring at the car's beam?
What if I never existed?
This life is a night terror.
What if I never existed?
Everyone would be okay
Because if I never existed,
I'd never have to stay.

— Lizzy Travis

THE PANDEMIC AND THE SENSITIVE ONES

FOR THE PAST six months, we have battled so much unrest and a pandemic, on top of it all. For weeks, we were ordered to quarantine ourselves in our homes, and only the essential workers were allowed on the roads. Socializing was only done through social media. Politics is at its peak, with a new election on the rise in just a few months. The battles and mudslinging have been penetrating the television, newspapers, and social media, bringing anxiety and fighting full steam. Riots and shootings are all over the country. Some whom we thought were good and trusting are showing their true colors and tarnishing the trust and reputation of the men and women we need to protect us. The innocents are being killed by the hour. People are dying by the thousands because of the pandemic. The division of America has taken over, and love and peace have been forgotten. Negative energies and emotions have blanketed the earth.

The empathic/sensitive ones are absorbing the tension and emotions of everything that has been unleashed. The sensitive ones feel it, and when I say "feel it," I mean it *hurts*, physically hurts. Families are struggling financially because many jobs have been closed, which is creating more built-up energy within the household. The empathic/sensitive children start to unconsciously and automatically mimic the emotions and actions of others who encompass their world. They start acting out, bouncing off the walls, having emotional overload and breakdowns regularly. These children who have been unrecognized as highly sensitive have porous boundaries, and with their giving and compassionate nature, they find themselves wanting to fix or protect the ones they love. They are so highly attuned to the emotions and energy of others that they go into emotional overload trying to rescue their loved ones. Their brains act as if they are experiencing whatever others are feeling. When they cannot fix it, they too dwell on it and somehow feel that it is their fault. "Mommy is crying. I cannot make her happy. I cannot make her smile and be happy. Daddy is not working. He is mad and frustrated. Mommy and daddy are fighting. It is my fault." Can you ever imagine how chaotic it is for your sensitive child, not knowing which feelings are their own and which are someone else's and still having love and compassion for all who are in their life and the world? Can you even imagine? Can you imagine all this going on inside your child, and no one, even the child, knows or understands? It is scary and, to some, devastating and traumatic. During this world crisis and breakdown, some are locked away in abusive homes and trapped in codependent relationships with no escape.

These highly sensitive children are on a roller coaster of emotions, and their self-esteem is bottoming out. Parents do not know how to handle them. Their fear that something is seriously wrong with their children start a panic within them. Their children are bouncing off the walls, and these parents are pulling their hair out. This is all due to overload. *Breathe!*

Many highly sensitive people and empaths like being by themselves and often stray from crowds because they feel uncomfortable around certain types of people and because they do not want to be discovered and judged. The undiscovered just feel confused without reason. This chaos is hurting them, and they feel caged. Hospitals are filled with children who try and hurt themselves, or they get violent or out of control. They get diagnosed with common ailments such as depression, ADHD, or Asperger's, get medicated, and are sent home. Has anyone ever wondered why there is such an epidemic of these conditions, even during a pandemic? More people need to open their minds and eyes and start asking these questions.

Escalated Struggles during Isolation

What are overlooked are the struggles that the highly sensitive deal with during this time. Their emotions can be flipped like a light switch without warning, often expressed with rage. This causes them to be labeled and judged by their peers, looked down upon, or isolated from those whom they call their friends. This all causes their mood to accelerate because of being noticed for their mood flips. Since they do not know how to control these mood flips, they themselves feel embarrassed, and it brings up other emotions, such as feeling vulnerable, depressed, and misunderstood. They crawl into a hole. They feel more deeply than the mainstream person. Every emotion is felt with deep passion, with such intensity. They care a lot about everything, which can leave the empath affected for days from just one disagreement, comment, or event.

They get manipulated and deceived by narcissistic and toxic people. This is a trap for compassionate empaths. They want to see the good in all; therefore, they bypass their intuitive ability to identify dishonest people or those who are not of good faith and end up trapped in a narcissistic relationship or friendship. In the end, the sensitive ones are upset with themselves for not listening to their gut, which they knew to be true from the start, but they wanted to see the good in all or give the benefit of the doubt. Empaths know if someone is good or bad, so trying to see the good in all or giving the benefit of the doubt does not exactly apply. One handshake or one hug could give them everything they know about a person. No secrets are hidden from them. Highly sensitive/empathic ones are not bound by social graces because their abilities do not lie.

Empaths struggle with the immediate knowing when someone is off. This was a hard one for me. I would always know when someone in my family was off and would ask what was wrong, and every time I would get "I am fine. Nothing's wrong." I knew there was something wrong, and it would eat at me, and I would have anxiety about it. I cannot let it go. Soon, my good day would become bad because I absorbed their emotions. In the end, days later, it would come out that indeed, something was wrong, which, if it were said days ago, would have saved me much anguish and would have been days in the past. Self-doubt is a common struggle for empaths because half the time, they do not know if it is them or if it is someone else. As a medium and an empath, I always go through this moment of self-doubt before I do a reading, and many times, it lasts until just before the reading, when the first message is received and given. I am always amazed by the end of the reading because it is all validated. Through the years, I have learned to blow off self-doubt and classify it within me as a false emotion.

Empaths need to take time to themselves. This can be one of the biggest struggles and never understood by others. We live life today in a fast-paced world, with most people having families. Their lives can be chaotic, with so much indecision, too much drama, and no real ground. Life is surrounded daily with all these energies that at the peak of all this, they need to have a moment or two to themselves. Sometimes a retreat is needed. When I walk into some places with children bouncing off the walls, elevated voices, and loud music, I feel like I am walking into a warzone without any armor. As a highly sensitive person, I feel the energy and vibration through my body. If you are not trained and prepared, this sudden shift in energy and vibration can come at you like a freight train, propelling you into a spiral. This happens to me. Think of what it could do to your empathic child, who is unaware of what is happening.

As empaths are being quarantined, they are in close proximity to all family members, and finding a place to just be alone, to escape, is a need. The television is filled with death and violence. The television alone gives off so much energy into the already chaotic household, which also contributes to the highly sensitive person's overload. They want to do something, but they cannot do something they do not enjoy because they will feel like they are in some way lying, and that hurts physically. They become bored, and that boredom accelerates to a level that they cannot control. Many will go into a tailspin and panic; panic turns into a meltdown. Calming them down is hard at this point. Touching them makes it worse; they do not want to be touched, but leaving them alone can be dangerous. Your anxiety and stress can make them explode. The highly sensitive feel every vibration. *Breathe!* Shhh.

My recommendation at this point is to turn off all video games, television sets, any stimulating electronics. Start playing soft meditation music. Take a deep breath, in and out. Exhale once and hard to release, blowing out all the bad. Then the rest should be slow breathing with some slow body movements like I talked about earlier in this book. Qigong is my go-to (an ancient Chinese exercise and healing technique to help with the movement of energy, involving meditation and controlled breathing and movement) and EFT tapping therapy (a combination of ancient Chinese acupressure and modern psychology), which send calming signals to your brain. This, combined with the energies of the crystals and stones, create a combination that will help move the stagnant energy and release it as well as charge the body and protect it from the absorption of other people's energies. Some say, "Um, right. My kid will not do that." They will if you set these boundaries and patterns. You will change the energy the moment the music starts, and your child will start the releasing process.

Battling the situation with an overloaded highly sensitive or empathic child with anger and frustration only creates a more volatile situation. They need to balance the mind, body, and soul by harnessing their strength and energy and creating solid energetic boundaries to stop these random fluctuations. By doing this, they unveil their authentic spiritual selves to themselves and one day to the world. The people your child is exposed to are very essential. Although the world is full of different mindsets and personalities, as humans, we are supposed to accept and not judge people for who they are, but that does not always happen in the real world, and the people you want exposed to your highly sensitive/empathic child are people who do not want to change or use them. These are people who do not put down who they are because it does not fit into their mainstream belief system, who will not badger them to come out of their shell, berate them, or ignore them. Acceptance and people who take them seriously keep the highly sensitive from living lives of fear, shame, and pain that can lead them to drugs or alcohol for escape and to ease the pain or make them feel anxious, depressed, and numb.

With acknowledgment and acceptance, highly sensitive or empathic children can grow to be the inspired visionaries who will open our eyes and bring us back to our authentic selves, where we can change the energy of the world, not just accept life the way it is, and end this chaos and destruction, bringing us back to love. It all begins with the first sign—when they say, "Mommy, when I was big," and when they tell you about their journey home and the lessons of lifetimes before.

TRISH AVERY

JUST LIKE ME

I DID NOT WRITE this book from just research that stemmed from the books in the bibliography. I wrote this from firsthand knowledge. I wrote this from my emotional and physical experiences. I grew up in foster homes. I say "homes" because I was not one of those children who were picked and lived with their forever families. I was different and too much to handle, and as I got older, it did not change. I was on my own at fifteen years old. I needed to live life my way. I went through life searching for answers as to who I was. It took me half my life to connect the dots, to balance my empathic soul.

It was not until I had found people in my life who supported me and acknowledged me for who I was, with only intrigue and not with judgment, people who let me be me and gave me the room to discover my authentic self, that I was able to connect the dots. Like everything else, self-discovery was not an easy task, and to achieve it, I had to drop all my defenses and let go of all the labels that had been inflicted upon me by others that I took on as being truths. I had to redefine the conditions and textbook diagnosis of who I am and why. I had to look within.

I was that person who used anger destructively, always looking for that thrill to take away or pacify the pain and confusion I held deep inside me. Sometimes I fell into deep depression, not getting out of bed for days. One time, when I was moved from one foster home that I thought would be my forever home, I did not speak a word for months. No one could get me to talk, not even a counselor. I have, through my life, been on upswing moods one minute and downswing moods the next, and I have been diagnosed with ADHD and major depression and anxiety, even PTSD. I have been seconds away from ending my life. I was the "rebel without a cause," but I am not. I never wanted to be any of those things. I was misunderstood and labeled many different things, such as "belligerent," "attention seeker," "weird," "bipolar," and "overly sensitive," just to name a few, but I was none of those things. I was me, misunderstood and unrecognized. I was and am an empath.

My saving graces were my deep desire to know why things were what they were and my obsessive love for books. My other asset was that I was a listener and an observer. I looked for the right answer that fit, not just an answer that was politically correct or that fit into society's box. I recognized myself in my search. I felt it through every level of emotion, discovering who I am sometimes by reading a chapter in a book from people who had researched people like me—and I thought I was alone. As life went on, I discovered my authentic self and learned how to balance and live a "normal" life. I found techniques and exercises to help me. I became more confident in myself. I took off the mask that hid the real person.

The struggles to get to where I am today have been real, and as I look back at those years when I was lost and had no idea who I truly was, I am astounded that I conquered that mountain. As I connected the dots and unveiled my authentic self, I began to notice these same struggles in others. As my mask was wiped away, I began to be approached by other children who saw me and recognized me, and their parents would seek my help and understanding. Many of these children were either beginning puberty, where everything was at full speed and tripled in sensitivity, or close to puberty, and their parents were starting to see a bigger change. Prior to this, the parents just thought they had children who were unruly, but the mothers, with their instincts, started to sense something different. Some noticed their children's intuitiveness and feared this ability in their children for multiple reasons, from religious and cultural beliefs to just the fear of the unknown. I felt compelled to help these parents understand who they are and how to recognize their highly sensitive and empathic children.

The parents, at times, felt perplexed on how to raise and guide their highly sensitive/ empathic children. They needed to change their perspective and realize that they, as parents, have experiences and have experienced their inner lives and the outside world differently through different lenses on life than their own children.

These children are living in a world full of constant noise, high vibrations, and sensitive hearing. They are highly intuitive and are having trouble finding answers. They are just like me.

Listen to them.

AFTERWORD

*A quiet mind is one that is willing to speak
the truth that is felt internally.*

MY VISION IN writing this book was to open the eyes of the reader to help them understand themselves and, in turn, help their children be their authentic selves. There has been an abundance of parents who have been on the edge, trying to figure out what they call the strange actions of their children. They lie awake at night, wondering what is lurking around their children in the middle of the night, feeding them this strange information. They wonder why their children talk about other lives and "when they were big" when they have not even grown up yet. They wonder how they could know who Grandma is when Grandma passed away before they were born.

Some even talk about a being that plays with them and enrages mass fear in the hearts and minds of their parents but has no fear in their little children. They wonder why their children's emotions are out of the blue, sometimes with no reason, or why they have out-of-control breakdowns and bounce off the walls. They wonder why they scream and hide when they see or meet other people or why certain places or rooms make them scared or timid. Mainstream thinkers shout, "Demons!" and mention angry spirits and possessions. Doctors and other professionals claim several disorders.

In this book, I have given you another perspective that I hope you take to heart. Through my work, I have genuinely enjoyed working with these children and listening to their stories of "when they were big." Opening this door showed me that "When I was big" is only the beginning. As I watched and listened to each one, I recognized my own story. Not being mainstreamed and human grounded into a strict belief system, I could remember and relate to my own younger years, and I relished in the memories of my youngest son's memories from his connections that he still, at twenty-two, has.

Many parents whom I have talked to when they are awakened to this perspective talk about being sad when the stories fade and wonder how some keep the connection and why it does fade. My answer is that it is not nurtured, and mainstream beliefs are allowed to be thrown into the mix. Parents fear their children being weird and being bullied, and their authentic selves get masked. We as humans worry about being politically correct and keeping up with the people around us so we fit in and not just be who we are. The authentic self fades.

In my first book, *Through the Cracks: The Magic in Me*, I narrated my childhood, where a closet was my babysitter. I was just three years old, and I had managed to survive it. These events were common in my childhood, and I often wondered how I could have survived those years. I would hear people say to me, "God was watching over you." Since I have always been a traveler between worlds, that has never been my belief. I've never believed in God as the one person shining down upon us. My belief lay deeper than that. I believe that God is in all of us. We are God and create our own path. I believe that we are souls within bodies and that our higher consciousness is our essence, what people call God. Life, death, and rebirth are the circle and journey of life. We learn new lessons in every lifetime and have guides, spiritual beings, angels, whatever you want to call them, to help guide us if we are willing to listen. They are part of our spiritual family.

As I started writing and working with others and their children, I found that their memories were like mine. Their purely innocent memories, untouched or unmasked by mainstream beliefs, were like mine. It took me years to connect all the dots, but a three-to-four-year-old had all that knowledge. I enjoyed listening and watching them with such awe at each one's memories of their connection to their spirit and their past lives. The younger they were, the stronger the connection and the memory. As the years went by, I was able to see them grow; more abilities emerged, and their sensitivity and empathic, intuitive gifts presented themselves, un-nurtured and unacknowledged. As puberty starts at around the age of nine, chaos starts with too much change and too many energy cycles going through this little human. Disaster starts. With this book, I hope I gave you the tools to help you and your highly sensitive or empathic child through this. My intention was not to change your belief system but to give you another perspective, to open your eyes and ears so you can hear your children from the beginning as they teach us about life and tell us the truth of where we came from and who we are within.

It has been an amazing experience for me to watch my own grandchildren come into this world and see them connect to this earthly life once again, squirming their way through the first few months, getting used to their new bodies so they can continue their journey. I listen eagerly to their long-awaited coos as they smile and tell me of their adventures, waiting for the day they come into words I can understand. It has been heartwarming to watch my one-year-old granddaughter raise her arms at a picture to be picked up as she talks to the picture of her deceased great-grandmother, who passed four years before she was born, or at times listen to her as she is talking and no one is around. When I ask her who she is talking to, she point to her great uncle on the wall, whose was killed in a motorcycle accident nine years past. It is amazing to hear my four-year-old grandson talk about when he was big and died and woke up born again and watch him do things he was never taught in this lifetime to do as he says, "Mommy, I did that when I was big."

I hope you enjoyed reading this book and that it helped you understand what may be going on with your children and answered all your questions as to why your children talk and act this way. I hope you find peace within you and that it helps you discover the love and beauty that is unmasked as the authentic self shines through. If acknowledged, accepted, and raised in honor of their authentic selves, these children will push humanity into its next phase: love without persecution and judgment. They are a reflection of who humans are meant to be and what they can do. Once they are acknowledged and you are not distracted by what everyone else's idea of reality is, they will show you how capable they really are.

When you hear, "Mommy, when I was big," smile and know it is only the beginning.

Acknowledge, accept, listen, nurture, and grow.

I am here to change the energy of the world from hate *to* love. *See me. Hear me. Feel me. Help me!*

I am me.
I don't pretend to be like everyone else.
I don't want to be like everyone else,
And I will not change who I am
Just to "fit in."
(www.TheLawofAttraction.com)

I am me. I see life through a different lens than you do. I am love.

Please feel free to review me on Amazon with five stars. It helps me, as an author, get my message out. You also can reach me at TrishAvery89@gmail.com.

APPENDIX

Stones and Crystals for Empaths and the Highly Sensitive

WEAR THEM, MEDITATE on them, or use them in grids.

Rose Quartz: For self-love, care, and harmony. Releases the past and soothes emotional wounds.

Amethyst: Rebalancing, protection. Alleviates anxiety, fatigue, and stress. Boosts psychic ability and intuition by opening the third eye. Used in meditation to gain a higher state of consciousness. Its higher vibration protects your energy field.

Black Obsidian: Helps see the truth. Blocks psychic attacks, provides energy protection, and dispels negativity. Provides a barrier from outside influences and emotionally negative and needy people.

Blue Quartz: Amplifies healing, intuition, empathy, and clarity and enhances clear and open communication.

Fluorite: Stabilizes and protects the aura. Deflects electromagnetic smog and stress. Also helps create and keep healthy boundaries, neutralizing harmful and negative energies.

Black Tourmaline: Keeps negative energies away and protects the empath from absorbing energy. The number-one stone for an empath. Keep a piece in your pocket.

Hematite: Strongest for grounding. Strengthens your aura, repels negative vibrations, calms emotions, and acts as a reflective shield.

Smoky Quartz: Transmutes negative energy and detoxifies the environment and the body. Helps you let go of feelings, thoughts, and emotions not in your best interest.

Calcite: Toxic in its raw form. Clears and releases stagnant energy, restores balance, and strengthens your sense of compassion. Enhances intuition. Clear this stone regularly.

Lepidolite: Helps reduce the absorption of stress and anxiety from others. Filters outside influences and restores emotional balance.

Colors and the Empath

Colors represent certain emotional and physical vibrations in our bodies. Empaths can feel and visualize colors because each color has a vibrational energy that affects their emotions. They each vibrate at a different frequency. To an empath, they have their own density and pulse and can be perceived as a color, a sound, and a feeling.

- **Red:** Survival, passion, raw power/energy, health
  Chakra: Root — strength, physical energy, stability, power
- **Orange:** Romantic love, joy, happiness
  Chakra: Sacral — sensuality, creativity, passion, sexuality
- **Yellow:** Power, health, confidence
  Chakra: Solar Plexus — pure energy, clarity, joy, optimism
- **Green:** Unconditional love
  Chakra: Heart — nature, equilibrium, life, growth
- **Light Blue:** Spoken truth, creativity
  Chakra: Throat — truth, intelligence, freedom
- **Indigo:** Intuition
  Chakra: Third Eye — inner depths, intuition, wisdom, devotion
- **Lavender:** Spirituality
  Chakra: Crown — dreams, the imagination, purity, innocence, illumination

Angels associated with Empaths

For those who work and associate with angel energy, there are a few who work with empaths:

Archangel Gabriel — They have healing rays for developing your intuition.

Angel Phuel — They help you balance out your emotions when you are overwhelmed.

Archangel Muriel — This angel is the patron angel of empaths. They are the angel of intuition and emotional harmony. This angel connects through clairalience, a form of psychic communication through the sense of smell. When you smell strange, out-of-place smells like smoke or flowers, take notice and listen. You are receiving information from the spiritual realm. This angel is part of the order of angels known as the Dominions and is part of the second angelic sphere. They awaken compassion and love in our hearts. To call upon Muriel, gather and hold a bouquet of flowers, face the south, and repeat the angel's name many times. Once you're calm and still, make your request to Muriel. This patron angel helps teach you about your intuition by trusting your intuitive guidance.

- **Suggested Meditations** *Einstein's Dream* (Monroe Institute)
- *Guide to Serenity* (Monroe Institute)
- *Angels, Fairies, and Wizards: A Magical Healing for Children* (Girl and Boy Versions) (Carmen Montoto)
- *The Return* (Micah Sadigh)

Doctors and Professionals in This Field

There are many doctors and professionals in this field, and I can only name a few of my favorites whom I endorse and respect from their work in this field:

- Dr. Brian Weiss, MD
- Meg Blackburn Losey, PhD
- Carol Bowman, MS
- Judith Orloff, MD
- Dr. Joe H. Slate
- Dr. Ian Stevenson
- Jim B. Tucker, MD
- Dr. Wayne Dyer

BIBLIOGRAPHY

The Children of Now — Meg Blackburn Losey, PhD

Soul's Journey: The Story of Traveling through Time to Find the Truth — G. C. DePietro

Old Souls — Tom Shroder

Life before Life: Children's Memories of Previous Lives — Jim B. Tucker, MD

Return to Life: Extraordinary Cases of Children Who Remember Past Lives — Jim B. Tucker, MD

Faded: The Circle of Life to the Soul — Trish Avery

Where Reincarnation and Biology Intersect — Ian Stevenson

The Transformation: Healing Your Past Lives to Realize Your Soul's Potential — Ainslie MacLeod

The Children of Now Evolution — Meg Blackburn Losey, PhD

Children's Past Lives: How Past Memories Affect Your Child — Carol Bowmen

We All Have Souls, and I Think We Can Prove It — Tom Blaschko

Life after Life — Raymond A. Moody Jr., MD

Handbook to Higher Consciousness — Ken Keyes Jr.

The Big Book of Reincarnation: Examining the Evidence That We All Lived Before — Roy Stemman

Life beyond Death: What Should We Expect? — David Fontana

Beyond Reincarnation: Experience Your Past Lives and Lives In Between — Joe H. Slate, PhD

The Children That Time Forgot — Mary and Peter Harrison

Children of the World: A Guide to the Coming Changes in Human Consciousness — P. M. H. Atwater, LHD

The Instruction: Living the Life Your Soul Intended — Ainslie MacLeod

Same Soul, Many Bodies — Dr. Brian Weiss

The Akashic Records Made Easy: Unlock the Infinite Power, Wisdom, and Energy of the Universe — Sandra Anne Taylor

Opening the Akashic Records: Meet Your Record Keepers and Discover Your Soul's Purpose — Maureen J. St. Germain

Parenting the Children of Now: Practicing Health, Spirit, and Awareness to Transcend Generations — Meg Blackburn Losey, PhD

The Empath's Survival Guide: Life Strategies for Sensitive People — Judith Orloff, MD

The Highly Sensitive Empath: How to Stop Overload, Find Your Sense of Self, and Thrive in an Overwhelming World — Theresa Evans

Evolutionary Empath: A Practical Guide for Heart-Centered Consciousness — Rev. Stephanie Red Feather, PhD

Thriving as an Empath: 365 Days of Self-Care for Sensitive People — Judith Orloff, MD

The Spiritual Power of Empathy: Develop Your Intuitive Gifts for Compassionate Connection — Cyndi Dale

Conversations with the Children of Now — Meg Blackburn Losey, PhD

Return from Heaven: Beloved Relatives Reincarnated within Your Family — Carol Bowmen

Memories of Heaven: Children's Astounding Recollections of the Time before They Came to Earth — Dr. Wayne W. Dyer and Dee Garnes

Living the Wisdom of the Tao: The Complete Tao Te Ching and Affirmations — Dr. Wayne W. Dyer

Through the Cracks: The Magic in Me — Trish Avery

Discover Your Soul's Path through the Akashic Records: Take Your Life from Ordinary to Extraordinary — Linda Howe

Lightning Source UK Ltd.
Milton Keynes UK
UKHW012014051120
372880UK00008B/421/J